DISCOVER *Your Value*
Your Purpose

ONE

My Testimony

I have always considered myself to be a good person. I went to church when I felt like it. I paid my taxes. I was polite and well-mannered. I graduated from college. I had a good job, family, and friends. On the surface I was a "good" person—but in reality, I was hiding from myself and others who I really was. Under all of the bravado and illusions of self-confidence, I was angry, wounded, bitter, selfish, and confused about my place in life.

I did not know my value or who I really was; and I often found myself in all kinds of places, doing all kinds of things, with all kinds of people. Because I did not know my value— what I was worth—I thought I was doing good living by the world's standards. Even so, subconsciously I knew there was more. There was something inside of me, in my spirit, which kept surfacing and drawing me. The problem was that back then I never really wrapped my mind around what this inner desire was. I never took the time to step back and look at my life and the consequences of my actions. I filled my life with people, material things, and activities that I thought were the answer to my lingering feelings of discontent. Of course, there were some moments when I was pacified, but nothing really changed. I still knew something was not right; I just did not know how to discover what was bothering me.

I am the oldest of three children. I have one brother and a sister. I was raised in a good middle-income family by two parents who loved and raised me the best they could. I was well taken care of, never abused, and did well in school. But I grew up feeling left out, rejected, misunderstood, and emotionally detached.

As a young child, I was very sensitive; until finally, my feelings of rejection took root in my spirit. I then became an angry child and an angry adult, carrying the baggage of rejection. I did not love myself and I did not understand I had value beyond what the world prescribed for me.

An angry adult Brinda made choices based on the world's standards, choices that should have helped me feel better about myself. I read self-help books, sought out people for advice, got married, got divorced, graduated from college, worked hard to advance my career, started a business, had two babies out of wedlock, and got married again. Some of these choices made me feel better for a while, some made me miserable, one caused a great loss, some made me tired, some wasted my time and money, and some gave me love and joy—but ultimately, none pacified the lingering desire in my spirit, a force that was pulling me in an unknown direction.

As a young child, I could sense the presence of God about me and I remember feeling free and blessed. Every person senses the presence of God. You can say otherwise, but I know and you know that you have, at some point in your life, sensed God's presence. My problem, and I suspect it is your problem as well, is trying to hear God through all of the distractions of life.

As a child and as an adult, I felt rejected and wounded and

kept looking for ways to fill that void. I wanted love. We all want to feel as someone loves us. The human desire for love never goes away. When I could not get the authentic love I sought, I looked for other ways to fill the void. Those distractions gave me a false value and a distorted purpose in life.

I know I am not the only person who is broken. I see people looking for love, value, and purpose every day. I see the brokenness in people: in the crimes that are committed, the violence that has taken over our communities, the killings, the abuse, the discrimination, health issues, deviant sexual behavior, and the content and tone of our communication with each other. These extreme behaviors are distractions that keep people from discovering God's love and their true value and purpose in life.

VALUE AND PURPOSE

I have discovered my value and my purpose. My value is that I am a child of God. He allowed His Son to die for my sins; and in doing so, all of my sins have been forgiven and I now belong to the Kingdom of God.

My purpose in this life is to get you to understand that you have value and purpose beyond your everyday life and challenges. God loves you and created you for a purpose. There it is! **YOU** were created for God's purpose. **YOU** are not your own.

We all have a life. My life is my family, my friends, and my job. I am a mother, a wife, a daughter; and I have a career in real estate—but they are not my purpose. They are things I do. They are not the purpose that God has for me.

The purpose God created me for has nothing to with the career I have chosen (you may be different) or the situations I have gone through. The purpose God created me for (and I may discover other purposes later), is to get you to understand that God loves you and that He created you to serve His purpose.

I know you have things to do, but that is not your purpose. I know you have gone through some experiences that have left you feeling tired and hurt, but that is not where you belong. Your job is to complete the purpose God made you for before you die. Period. He made you and He can do with you what He wants. It doesn't matter what you want. What matters is what He wants because He made you. He planned how He was going to make you; so He knows everything about you. He created and formed you exactly the way He wants you to serve His purpose—not yours.

DISTRACTIONS

I am a sinner. I have sinned against every one of the Ten Commandments. I don't need to go into the details. Some I consciously chose to do; some I did not realize were sins until after I committed them.

It is easy to get caught up in this earthly life. There are so many ways we get distracted by our family, jobs, friends, and fear. I believe we are all searching for something—and that something is love.

But we make the mistake of looking for love in the wrong places. We look for and expect to find it in people and our possessions. As a child, I initially looked for love from my parents, grandparents, teachers, and friends. As an adult, I looked for love and acceptance from my boyfriends, my career, my business, my son, and in one of my marriages. When I could not find love in these distractions, in frustration and simplicity, I turned to sin to fill the void. What I thought was going to ultimately make me feel better, never did.

Looking back, I can now see that what I was really looking for was God. My problem was I was too distracted by my activities and emotions, I ended up unknowingly rejecting God and trying to create and live a life on my own. In essence, I sinned the original sin committed by the devil: I tried to be God.

When we try to build a life on our own, busy with our own self-interests, consumed with distractions and relying on own abilities, we are essentially trying to be God, which is how sin evolves.

A self-centered, busy life easily creates distractions. A life with no direction welcomes distractions. When I was busy, I didn't have time to focus on God or to think about my value and purpose. Why would I? I was too busy with my distractions, sinning and trying to be God.

Without God in my life, I left the door open for distractions—people I didn't need to be around, spending too much money, not making wise decisions, wasting my time, depression, pride, and sexual sins.

We all have different ways to express our frustration when we cannot find love. The distractions we use to hide our frustration at not finding love manifest into all kinds of sins: abuse, lying, fornicating, adultery, prostitution, stealing, murder (physical and spiritual), using people, selfishness, sexually deviant behaviors, embezzlement, mischief, gossiping, cheating, being prideful, drug and alcohol abuse, gambling, excessive debt, and so on. All of these sins (and others not mentioned) point to behaviors of people looking for love, not finding it, and then turning (away from seeking love) to sin to fill that void (trying to be God).

All sin can be avoided when we seek a relationship with God.

SUBMISSION

For years, I sought out relationships with people, things, and activities. Finally, at the age of fifty-one, I discovered that what I was trying to do was not working and that I was distracted.

In August 2014, I reached a point where I had no more options. I was under a lot of stress at work and the city I lived in experienced a flooding, so practically everything in my basement was soaked or exposed to wastewater and had to be thrown out. The other two-thirds of the basement was either moved to the first floor of my house or placed outside. And, over the course of three weeks, the entire basement was infested with mold and had to be demoed, decontaminated and reconstructed.

Now, to give you some context, I have a controlling personality and I hate clutter. So, for about four months, I was living in a cramped, mold-infested house, trying to find a contractor to remove the mold and reconstruct the basement, and money to pay for it all. In the end, I had to take out a FEMA loan and use money from my 401k to reconstruct the basement. Borrowing money on a house I no longer wanted, just drove me up the wall.

Remember, I had anger problems *before* the flood, so you know I was cuckoo for Cocoa Puffs with the flooding and the reconstruction of the basement—especially with my other responsibilities of going to work (stressful job) and being a wife, and mother.

One day, I think it was in November 2014, I came home from work and, as I did every day since the flood, went downstairs to assess the basement. When I got downstairs, my thoughts were everywhere: on the mold that was still growing on the wall studs and ceiling like crazy, on all the money I was spending, on how much more money I needed to borrow, on how long the work was taking, on how I was never going to be able to sell the house and move.

It went on and on. I was miserable and the devil was talking to me daily, taking full advantage of my situation and weaknesses. As a controlling person, I like options. However, I found that with the basement, I had no options. The mold was getting worse and I didn't know if my family and I should just walk away from the house. On top of all of that, there was stress at the job and at home. I realized my back was up against a wall and I had done all I could do—so I just gave up.

At the bottom of the basement stairs, I confessed, "Here, Lord. Just take it, just take my problems. I give you all my problems to solve. I tried, but I can't do it; so I am giving it all to you." Instantly, after giving my burdens to God, I felt a weight lifted from me and God started to work on my behalf. But before

I could walk away, the Holy Spirit prompted me and I realized there was something else that I needed to give God. I needed to give God my life. I needed to offer my life as a sacrifice to Him—and at that moment, I gave my life to God.

All this time, I was afraid to give God control over my life. As I walked away, the Holy Spirit inserted Himself into my thoughts and gave me the revelation that it never was my life to begin with, it was always God's.

Wow! What a powerful revelation. All these years, I thought I was in control, building my life and living the way I wanted to with my distractions. The distractions got so big I could not see God. I could always sense Him, but I allowed the distractions and sins to separate me from a relationship with Him.

GOD IS INTENTIONAL

It is funny that when we think things are going well in life, we don't make God our first thought. Oh, but when trials come, we are much more receptive to that small, still voice. The more I learned about God in my Bible studies, the more I realized how much He loves me. In God's love, I learned how awesome and magnificent He is, how powerful and creative. He is sovereign, He is All in All, Alpha and Omega, the Beginning and the End, the Creator of the universe and all things in it.

But, I also discovered He is personal and intentional. He thought of me in all His creations. He planned how I would look, what I would say, and how I would behave. He created me. He knew me, not just in passing, but He knew me. He included me in His forever plans. He saw me as His creation and He saw me as who I should be: a reflection of Him.

I have seen and experienced an inkling of His love for me, which is way more expansive than I can ever express. He saw me for who I was: someone who was broken, wounded, and weak and looking for His love. He accepted me as I am. In all of His wonder and greatness, I fell in love with God. And, in love, I submitted my life back to Him (it was really His all along anyway). Now, in my love for Him and my acknowledgment that He loves me, I am open to hearing and doing what He wants. Now, in my love for God, I can see my weaknesses and the distractions that hinder my relationship with Him.

God did not reveal all of my distractions at once. No, the first revelation I had was actually before I totally sacrificed my life to Him. It came one day when Pastor Larry, my pastor, said in a sermon that some people are in mourning and never even know it. His words stuck with me and I began to wonder if I was in mourning.

Well, I was in mourning because I felt rejected in some proportion from my parents. Even though I knew they loved me, I believed their version of love was expressed at a distance. This device of the devil ingrained itself in my spirit, my will, my mind, and everything that I did.

Looking back, I can now see this spirit of rejection manifested in my life. I was rebellious and always in trouble with my parents. I always had a bad attitude, talked back, was promiscuous, selfish, insecure, prideful, impatient, and angry. After reflecting, I asked myself why I got angry. Why did I get all worked up over things and people? It was revealed to me that I was angry because I thought someone was trying to take something from me. Every one of these behaviors was a reflection of me being angry and believing that someone was trying to take something from me because I did not feel I had received love. In my frustration, I turned to distractions that led me to sin.

Once I had the revelation of the cause of my anger, I realized that my heavenly Father provides for all of my needs. I didn't have to worry about anything being taken from me because my God is my heavenly Father; and He is also my Daddy and He provides for me. If I want something, all I have to do is ask in faith and believe.

I asked the Lord to bind my anger on earth and to take it from me. Instantly, I felt a weight lifted off my body, my spirit, and my mind. I was no longer an angry person. Hallelujah! Years of rejection and anger immediately lifted off of me.

Now, that does not mean I am not perturbed from time to time—but I am no longer an angry person. God has lifted that weight and I can now move closer to the purpose He has for me in this life. God is my first priority and I recognize that when the devil is trying to distract me, I need to maintain my focus on God's love.

Denial is Dangerous

Denial of your distractions is dangerous. Distractions will connect you with people you should avoid. Distractions will put you in debt buying more than you can use or afford. Distractions will cause you to hate and mistreat others. Distractions will make you a parent before marriage. Distractions will come between you and your covenant with your spouse and God. Distractions will lead you to abuse your child or spouse. Distractions will lead you to prison. Distractions will have you engaged in sex before marriage. Distractions will have you entangled in deviant sexual behavior. Distractions will make you a liar and a cheater. Distractions will make you a rapist or a murderer. Distractions will tell you to curse someone out. Distractions will proclaim you have no value and lead you to depression or suicide. Distractions will make you abuse drugs or alcohol. Distractions will cause sickness and death. Distractions will detour you away from God's purpose for your life.

Distractions are powerful tools of the devil. The devil is real and he has power on this earth. The devil (originally called Lucifer) is sneaky and often wrapped up in someone or something you desire and long for. The devil was not always as he is now. Originally, Lucifer was created in perfection. He was an anointed cherub (set aside for God's purpose), full of wisdom (a way of thinking and conduct that is orderly, socially sensitive, and morally upright), perfect in beauty (covered in every precious stone and gold), a guardian of God's throne, great (had the highest position of all of God's creations), a musician, and a creature with free will. Initially, Lucifer performed his purpose, but his intellect, authority, and beauty led him to feel superior to God; and he eventually decided he was going to make himself God and take over Heaven. Lucifer's iniquity (sin, wickedness) is that he no longer wanted to be God's servant and complete the purpose he was created to do. Instead, he wanted to be served (worshiped).

God called Lucifer out in his wickedness and clearly described that his sins began with his prideful feelings about himself, and in turn, those feelings corrupted his wisdom and drove him to wickedness. Lucifer freely chose to let his gift of wisdom be perverted by his competitive attitude (comparing himself to God), his discontent (not being content with his purpose), and his pride (I am better than God), which resulted in sin and violence.

We know what happened next. The devil and one-third of the angels (Lucifer spread his sin to the other angels) went to war with God in Heaven; they were defeated and cast out of Heaven, down to earth, because the devil did not want to complete the purpose God had created specifically for him. Lucifer chose to become Satan, the devil, by going outside of God's purpose and allowing sin to mold his character.

Now, the devil has created his own purpose, to oppose all that is good, right, and godly. And just like he spread his message of wickedness to one-third of God's angels, the devil lied to Adam and Eve and distracted them from God's purpose for their lives. Adam and Eve had everything they needed in the Garden of Eden and God had given them their purpose and authority to rule the earth, but they were easily distracted and willfully committed the original sin also committed by Lucifer: they wanted to be God. Their wisdom was perverted and they sinned by following the devil's lead; and in doing so, sinned and gave their authority to the devil. The perversion of God's will (sin) started with Lucifer, then was accepted by one-third of God's angels, then became an uninvited distraction to Adam and Eve, and now it resides in all of us.

The devil does not have to think of a multitude of ways to draw us to sin (distractions) and away from our original relationship with God, he doesn't have to because the original sin he used—I want to be God worked on a third of God's angels, worked on Adam and Eve, and has been working marvelously on humans all these ages. There is no need for the devil to change the formula, which is: The devil lies to us. We believe it. We get distracted. We enter into sin and create distance between God and ourselves. We don't establish a relationship with God. We don't discover the purpose God created us for. And then we die.

You have been listening to the devil's lies. You have given him authority over your life—but you don't even know it. I know, you are probably thinking that you have a few issues, but you are still a good person and believe that God knows your heart; so that is your pass, your get-out-of-jail card. Those issues and the denial of your distractions are keeping you from establishing/re-establishing your relationship with God. They are preventing you from knowing how much He loves you and what He has planned for you.

Here are some issues you may be facing. Read them and see if any of them fit you. If they do, pay attention, because they are distracting you from establishing or strengthening your relationship with God.

+ Don't want anyone to tell you what to do.
+ Prideful.
+ Brag about what you have and how you have worked to get what you have.
+ People cannot talk to you without experiencing your bad attitude.
+ You think the world revolves around you and that your needs come before all others.

+ You constantly interrupt people when they are speaking.
+ You are impatient and want everything right now.
+ You are constantly busy doing nothing of real value.
+ Your person, house, and work area are dirty and constantly in a state of disorder.
+ You love money.
+ You are over your head in debt and have nothing substantive to show for it.
+ You have low self-esteem and you allow others to talk to and treat you however they want.
+ You hoard things or animals.
+ Your solution to a problem is revenge.
+ You engage in the use of illegal drugs or abuse prescription drugs or alcohol to the extent you are addicted.
+ You are jealous of others and measure yourself and what you have compared to them.
+ You are romantically involved and live with a person you are not married to.
+ You are married and engage in sex outside of your marriage.
+ You are not married and engage in sex with someone who is married.
+ You have sex outside of marriage.
+ You have sex with people of the same sex.
+ You engage in deviant sexual behavior (people, things, animals, situations).
+ You are abused by your mate or spouse.
+ You are the abuser in your relationship/marriage.
+ You are a compulsive liar.

+ You like to hurt people or animals.

+ You like starting arguments.

+ You like to manipulate people.

+ You never think you are wrong.

+ You like to control people and every situation.

+ You are overly critical of people.

+ You allow people to use you.

+ You are depressed and live with regrets.

+ You live in guilt for something you have done.

+ You were abused as a child.

+ You feel you were not loved or loved enough as a child.

The devil uses distractions like these examples to keep you from discovering how much God loves you, your value as God's child, and the purpose God has for you to complete in order to fulfill His purpose.

While doing research for this book, I came across a passage on the website www.gotquestions.org/purpose-of-life.html that summed up what my purpose and what your purpose is in this life. It reads:

> "Our purpose in life, as God originally created man, is 1) glorify God and enjoy fellowship with Him, 2) have good relationships with others, 3) work, and 4) have dominion over the earth. But with man's fall into sin, fellowship with God is broken, relationships with others are strained, work seems to always be frustrating, and man struggles to maintain any semblance of dominion over nature. Only by restoring fellowship with God, through faith in Jesus Christ, can purpose in life be rediscovered."

THIS MOMENT

The purpose of man is to glorify God and enjoy Him forever. We glorify God by fearing and obeying Him, keeping our eyes on our future home in Heaven, and knowing Him intimately. We enjoy God by following His purpose for our lives, which enables us to experience true and lasting joy—the abundant life that He desires for us.

As you read my testimony and thoughts about my journey to discovering my purpose in God, I hope you find something that reminds you of you, something that triggers a response in you to seek God's love, to discover your value and your purpose.

I wasted so much time living in denial of my distractions and chasing after people, ambitions, and things that did not matter. Before I take my last breath, my mind will not be focused on the clothes I wore, the cars I drove, the houses I lived in, my job title, money, or past relationships. My mind will not be on any of the things I was so preoccupied with when I was younger. My mind will be focused on God and my hope that I have completed the purpose He made and prepared for me.

In July 2015, at the age of fifty-two, I discovered my purpose. Through study in my church's Ambassador Bible Training School, I discovered my ministry gifts of discernment, administration, and teaching.

I struggled with discovering my purpose, until one day in July, the Holy Spirit revealed to me that my purpose is to tell people they have value and purpose beyond their everyday life, and that they need to discover their purpose in God.

I am not certain this is all God wants me to do, but for the moment, it is what He wants me to do, and it is being done as you read this book. I pray that God's Word and my testimony will open your mind and that your spirit will be receptive to answering God's call. He is calling for a moment such as this.

What about You?

You now know much about me. Now, it is time to discover more about you.

I asked a good friend of mine to read a draft of this book.

After reading it, she called to tell me what was on her heart and what the Holy Spirit was moving her to tell me. She said that as she was reading the draft, she felt a desire to write and interact with the manuscript. She thought it would be helpful if I provided some space after each chapter where readers could write down their thoughts and ideas.

My heart listened to her and the Lord directed me to Matthew 13:18-23, Luke 8:4-15, and Mark 4:3-20 where Jesus speaks in parable about what happens when seed (God's Word) falls on different types of ground. The parable describes four types of people who hear God's Word and how their responses to His Word produce an immediate impact on their lives.

The four types of people: Unresponsive, Impulsive, Preoccupied, and Believers are shown in the table on page 32. In Jesus's parable, he speaks of seed (God's Word) falling in different places (different conditions in the four types of people described). My purpose as a Believer is to tell you the great news, that God loves you, He created you for a purpose, and through the death and resurrection of his Son, Jesus Christ, you and I have value, power, and authority to complete the purpose God assigned to us before we die.

One of the ways I have been called to complete my purpose is to write this book. It is my desire that the seed (God's Word) from this book falls on "good ground"; that is, I want you to apply it (responsiveness) directly to your life.

Thus, at the end of each chapter you will find questions that will hopefully cause you to stop, think, reflect, write and then apply what was discussed in each chapter. I pray that the seeds that fall from this book fall on "good ground" and that you receive and respond to God's word in such a way that causes God's Word to multiply in your life by thirty, sixty, a hundredfold, or more.

Matthew 13:18-23, Luke 8:4-15 and Mark 4:3-20		
TYPES OF PEOPLE WHO HEAR THE WORD	PLACES WHERE THE WORD FALLS	RESPONSES TO GOD'S WORD
UNRESPONSIVE: Fail to respond to God's Word.	Wayside	Do not understand the Word that Jesus Christ is their Lord and Savior. The devil comes quickly and takes the Word away so they won't be saved.
IMPULSIVE: Superficial, emotional converts.	Stony	Hear the Word but have no foundation established. When troubles come, they return to their old ways and produce no fruit.
PREOCCUPIED: Carnal, worldly converts. Never break from their past.	Thorny	Hear the Word but allow worldly cares, deceitfulness of riches, material things, and lusts to take priority in their lives. They conform to the world and eventually any Word is choked out and they produce no fruit.
BELIEVERS: Respond to God's Word.	Good Ground	Hear the Word and they understand that Jesus Christ is their Lord and Savior. Because they understand, they produce fruit (understands how Jesus applies in their lives).

INTERACTIVE APPLICATION

1. Do you believe you are valuable and that God created you for a purpose?

2. Have you ever questioned your value?

3. Describe two or three significant emotional and/or physical hurts you have experienced.

4. Write down four positive and four negative words you would use to describe yourself.

5. Do any of the words you used to describe yourself reflect someone else's assessment of you? If so, write down which one(s) and the person(s) associated with the word.

6. Do you sense God's presence calling you?

7. Identify some obvious and not-so-obvious distractions in your life.

8. Originally, I visualized and understood the word *submission* to mean giving up power to make my own decisions. Do you feel the same or differently? If differently, describe how you define *submissive.*

9. Any thoughts you would like to remember later? If so, write them down here.

TWO

You Are Not an Accident— You Were Predestined by God

God created you for a purpose. At some point in time, God imagined and created you. From the top of your head to the bottom of your feet, every hair on your body, your smile, your disposition, your language, your skin color—God imagined and created it all.

Sometimes we say that a birth was not planned, but that is not true. God planned and created all of us, including you. Say it out loud: GOD CREATED ME!

He also gave you unique abilities, talents, and spiritual gifts that he wants you to use to edify Believers and to complete his purpose (1 Peter 4:10-11, Romans 12:6-8, Ephesians 4:11-16, Corinthians 12:7-11). Your talent might be your personality, communication skills, determination, generosity, wisdom, compassion, teaching skills, preaching skills, or anything else you are naturally good at.

Each of us has made something in our lives, like cooking a great meal, building cars, growing flowers, writing books, painting, and the like. Before chefs start to cook, they know what ingredients they will need and why they are cooking—so the food can be eaten. Before engineers build cars, they know what tools will be needed and why they are building it—for people to drive. The food and the car each have a purpose: to complete its creator's will—to be eaten and to be driven.

It is the same for us. God created you and me for a purpose to complete His will. I went through my life wasting time completing purposes that I conceived for myself. But the majority of those activities (distractions) had nothing to do with the reason God created me.

To counter my feelings of rejection and insecurity, I lived in fear and I allowed the values others placed on me to taint and cover my true value in God. It took a long time for me to feel some security in my person, but eventually I learned to love myself and to not be overly concerned about the opinions others had about me.

Eventually, I went 360 degrees and became so independent—I supported myself financially, paid for my college education, bought my own houses and cars, etc. During this time, I also believed that I made Brinda. But the insecurity was still there. The foundation I built my life on was shaky because it was built on my abilities. In Luke 6:48-49, Jesus speaks of houses being built on foundations of rock and not being shaken; and He speaks of houses built without foundations and when a flood strikes, the house collapses and is destroyed.

What foundation is your house—built on? Your money, job, education, relationships, children, marriage? None of these distractions give you value or purpose and none can make you whole and completely stable. They can give you a title and to-do lists to complete, but they are not your purpose. God created you and He has a purpose for you. God's desire and choice to create you ultimately resulted in the creation of an individual with value and purpose.

I particularly want to say to women: You will never find

your value in a relationship with a man. You must first find your value by establishing a relationship with God and with yourself. It is wonderful to be in a relationship and in love, to have a companion and do things together, to enjoy the blissfulness of connecting with someone sexually—I get that. But don't let a relationship with a man determine your value.

Don't let another person define, restrict, or abuse you.

Women are wired to be nurturers and to take care of people; often to the detriment of ourselves. If you are being verbally, mentally, or physically abused in your relationship (single or married), then you really need to hear this:

You have value and purpose beyond your everyday life.

You were not created to be dominated, used, beaten, abused, cursed at, or talked down to. If you are in this place, I know the devil is busy pushing those distractions in your face and pushing you into a box where you feel you cannot get out.

You can get out—but you have to choose "yes" and start eliminating the distractions the devil has devised to keep you bound by a life of fear. You have to realize that the devil knows you have value and that is why he works so hard to make you believe that you deserve to be bound, that the dysfunctional "love" you are receiving is justified because that is all that you deserve. No! You deserve much more!

Before you can get over that threshold, you have to believe it, and then move forward. Faith without work (movement, action) is dead (standstill, no life). This is not the time to rationalize away your distractions, now is the time to acknowledge your value.

You need to wrap your mind around the idea that God knew He was going to create you before you were even born. He saw your presence and already wrote your life (Psalm 139:13-17).

You are no accident. You were not created to be used, abused, beaten, or killed. You are fearfully and wonderfully made for His purpose. You have to seriously wrap your mind around this: God created you for His purpose. Period.

You may not like the idea. You may be afraid of the idea. You may be curious, or maybe you are excited. It doesn't matter. You must fulfill His purpose.

I heard that two of the best days in anyone's life are the day they are born and the day they discover the purpose that God has for them. I agree.

Get out of your everyday box and step forward into discovering God's purpose for your life.

Scripture to Reflect On

Below is a selection of Bible passages for your reading and reflection. I encourage you to read each Scripture noted in this book in a study Bible (a Bible that provides scholarly information designed to help the reader gain a better understanding of and context for the text), so you can gain additional revelation and encouragement. My personal Bible is *The King James Study Bible* by Thomas Nelson Publishers.

GENESIS 1:27 (ESV)
[27]So God created man in his own image, in the image of God He created him; male and female He created them.

ROMANS 8:29–30 (NKJV)
[29]For whom He foreknew, He also predestined *to be* conformed to the image of His Son, that He might be the firstborn among many brethren. [30]Moreover whom He predestined, these He also called; whom He called, these He also justified; and whom He justified, and these He also glorified.

PSALM 139:13–17 (ESV)

¹³For you formed my inward parts; you knitted me together in my mother's womb. ¹⁴I praise you, for I am fearfully and wonderfully made. Wonderful are your works; my soul knows it very well. ¹⁵my frame was not hidden from you, when I was being made in secret, intricately woven in the depths of the earth. ¹⁶Your eyes saw my unformed substance; in your book were written, every one of them, the days that were formed for me, when as yet there was none of them. ¹⁷How precious also are thy thoughts unto me, O God! How great is the sum of them!

JOHN 15:16 (NKJV)

¹⁶You did not choose me, but I chose you and appointed you that you should go and bear fruit, and *that* your fruit should remain, that whatever you ask the Father in My name He may give you.

EPHESIANS 2:10 (NKJV)

¹⁰For we are His workmanship, created in Christ Jesus for good works, which God prepared beforehand that we should walk in them.

PSALM 100:3 (ESV)

³Know that the Lord, He is God! It is he who made us, and we are his; we are his people, and the sheep of his pasture.

EPHESIANS 1:4–8 (NKJV)

⁴just as He chose us in Him before the foundation of the world, that we should be holy and without blame before Him in love, ⁵having predestined us to adoption as sons by Jesus Christ to Himself, according to the good pleasure of His will, ⁶to the praise of the glory of His grace, by which He made us accepted in the Beloved. ⁷In Him we have redemption through His blood, the forgiveness of sins, according to the riches of His grace ⁸which He made to abound toward us in all wisdom and prudence,

2 TIMOTHY 1:9 (NKJV)
[9]who has saved us and called *us* with a holy calling, not according to our works, but according to His own purpose and grace which was given to us in Christ Jesus before time began,

GALATIANS 1:15 (ESV)
[15]But when he who had set me apart before I was born, and who called me by his grace,

ACTS 17:26–27 (ESV)
[26]And he made from one man every nation of mankind to live on all the face of the earth, having determined allotted periods and the boundaries of their dwelling place, [27]that they should seek God, and perhaps feel their way toward him and find him. Yet he is actually not far from each one of us,

JOHN 3: 16–17 (ESV)
[16]"For God so loved the world, that he gave his only Son, that whoever believes in him should not perish but have eternal life. [17]For God did not send his Son into the world to condemn the world, but in order that the world might be saved through him.

EPHESIANS 1:11–12 (NKJV)
[11]In Him also we have obtained an inheritance, being predestined according to the purpose of Him who works all things according to the counsel of His will, [12]that we who first trusted in Christ should be to the praise of His glory.

REVELATION 4:11 (NKJV)
[11]"You are worthy, O Lord, To receive glory and honor and power; for You created all things, And by Your will they exist and were created."

ECCLESIASTES 12:7 (ESV)
[7]and the dust returns to the earth as it was, and the spirit returns to God who gave it.

INTERACTIVE APPLICATION

1. Write down your personal definition of *predestination*.

2. Now, grab your Bible or Google the Biblical definition of *predestination*. Is there a gap between your understanding of predestination and the Bible's definition? If so, what is it?

3. Is the life you live right now created by you or by God?

4. Can you see the original sin of trying to be God manifested in your life? If so, please describe.

5. Write down at least three examples from the past week when you stepped in and attempted to be God rather than seeking God first and doing his will.

6. Any thoughts you would like to remember later? If so, write them down here.

THREE

Works of the Flesh That Distract You from Seeking Your Purpose

The problem with me believing I was a good person is that it allowed me to live a life within a small box that I custom designed for myself. Since I made the box, I could put the walls up as high as I wanted, I could paint the box any color I wanted, and I could control what and who came into the box.

In that box, I was not completely happy; but I was comfortable and I was familiar with my environment; and most important, I believed I was in control of my life. In essence, I was trying to be God. My commitment to a life of denial and a mindset that I was "good" hindered me from living a life of purpose; and instead I lived a life of fear and complacency.

God did not give us the spirit of fear. Fear is a condition derived from the devil to keep us in a box with just enough to keep us comfortable. God created us with a purpose in mind and to walk with no fear in that purpose; not conform to a life we believe we created.

Denial is a very strong and persuasive spirit. I think denial is so strong because we prop it up with our pride and our fear—both of which are from the devil.

My biggest mistakes were dealing with and being in the company of people I knew I should not be around. A spiritual war was raging for my soul, but I was not even paying attention. Do you know why? Because I was distracted trying to create my own life and by being involved with people I should have walked away from.

The lack of love in a person's life can drive them to look for other means of comfort instead of the one true love they seek and need. My desire for love drove me into relationships that now, as I look back, I never should have been in. And, I thank God I did not remain in them. I was looking for the love I desired as a child and as an adult did not know existed with God.

I do not blame my parents. I know they love me and they did the best they could as they struggled with their own distractions while working and raising a family. I was never mistreated but there was always an emotional distance, a wall I could never manage to push down.

Children cannot understand the larger picture and dynamics of life. Children simply want love, security and support from their parents and other adults. When one or a combination of those are lacking in a child's life, there will eventually be emotional issues to address. What is said and done to children, both positive and negative will eventually show itself in a child's speech and behavior as they grow, mature, interact with others and more importantly, how they value themselves.

For me, that "emotional distance" from my parents, but particularly from my father caused me to be distant, rebellious, defensive, and argumentative. These same feelings and attitudes also permeated my adult life and relationships. I felt rejected; so I responded with negative behavior to get attention.

None of the negative attention I received from my behavior ever did me any favors. It only caused me to hunger for distractions, which of course led to a lifestyle of sin and created more distance between me and my God.

God cannot be in relationship with the unrighteous. You cannot live a lifestyle of sin and conform to this world and be in relationship with Him. You cannot serve two masters: God and the devil. You must choose one and commit.

God provides for the righteous and unrighteous. He provides all people (good and bad) with grace and mercies as we find our way out of our sinful lifestyles and back to him. But, let's be real. Our lives on earth are temporary. One day, we will die and if we are of the Christian faith, at death we will meet our Lord and Savior. The righteous (those who believe Jesus Christ is their Lord and Savior and died for their sins) will go to Heaven and see their Father. The unrighteous (those who did not listen and heed to that small, still voice calling them to establish a relationship with God and turn away from their lives of sin) will go to Hell.

It is very simple, but hard to understand because we try to rationalize what is not ours to rationalize. God created the Heavens and the earth and all that is in it. That includes me, you, us, them—all of us. He can do as He pleases because He is God, the Creator, the Protector, the Alpha, the Omega, the First, the Last. He is King, He is sovereign, and He is the Ruler of All. I could continue, but you get my point: He is the decision-maker.

We can be mad, bitter, ask questions and not believe—it does not matter, because in the end, it is all about God. He created us for His purpose. And He never forces us to do His will. He allows us time to choose to do His will; and if you choose to become His child, you will want to do His will.

Are works of the flesh distracting you? Is it your job? Your mate or your spouse? Your children? Preoccupation with material possessions? A bad relationship with a family member? Too many bills and not enough money? An unfulfilled dream? An abusive or controlling relationship?

There is a strong correlation between how you value yourself and the behavior you engage in. In Galatians 5:19-20, God provides us with a list of works of the flesh and tells us that those who practice such things will not inherit the Kingdom of God (be a child of God because you are distracted living your life, trying to be your own God).

If your lifestyle is based on any of the behaviors and activities noted below, you cannot expect to be born again, establish a relationship with God, be renewed in Christ, be a child of God, or be living a Christian lifestyle as an example of His Glory.

Initially, you may think none of the definitions or descriptions will fit you. But you may be surprised to find that one or even a few do fit and are behaviors that are blocking/hindering your relationship with God.

Adultery is defined as voluntary sexual intercourse between a married person and someone other than his or her lawful spouse. Marriage is a covenant between God, the husband, and the wife. There is no room in a marriage for a girlfriend or a boyfriend. And, just for clarity, a separated couple is still married and in covenant with God.

Fornication is defined as any kind of unlawful sexual intercourse, be it incest, prostitution, unchastity, homosexuality (sex with the same gender), bestiality (sex with animals), necrophilia (sex with a dead body), pedophilia (sex with children). All of these are deviant sexual behaviors. Some of these sins may be acceptable in our culture; however, they are still sins that separate us from a relationship with God, just like lying, stealing, or any other sin we indulge in. God did not create us to defile our bodies and our spirits, nor to harm others or animals or to engage in deviant sexual behavior. Our bodies belong to God, they were made to worship Him.

Uncleanness is defined as physical uncleanness or filth, ceremonial uncleanness (Matthew 23:27) and moral uncleanness.

This is not about keeping your body or home spotless; it is about letting filth invade and take over your spirit. Uncleanliness can start small, but eventually becomes something extreme as it takes over and you become a place maker for the filth (an example is hoarding).

Also, in my opinion, cursing has become a part of everyday speech as people use vile, negative words in common conversation. The speaker's intended use may not be derogatory; however, once spoken out loud, the meaning and power of the word still remains. Many of us engage in using curse words or are participants by allowing others to call us vile names (the N-word, B-word) without considering the effects such words have on those we speak to and our own spirits.

Lewdness is defined as unbridled lust, excess, licentiousness, lasciviousness, outrageousness, shamelessness, and insolence; wanton acts or manners, such as filthy words, indecent bodily movements, and unchaste handling of males and females; and the quality of being very sexual or lustful in an offensive way.

When I was growing up, there were standards and expectations of behavior. Now, as we have become a "me" society aimed to be transparent, it sometimes seems as if everything and anything is possible. Nothing shocks us anymore because we see everything on the Internet (YouTube, Facebook, Twitter, Instagram, etc.) and on TV and in the movies. I hear conversations with filthy words that were once said in close confidence to someone, but are now expressed openly.

Everything is over-the-top; people want more than they need and more than others have. People are living lifestyles of pushing the envelope to the edge. There is no modesty, no humbleness, no peace, and no quiet.

I sometimes wonder if this recklessness is driven by our spirits or by what we see on TV, in the movies, and on social media and we are simply trying to emulate. Women dress shamelessly, with their bodies casually out for display to the world.

Our bodies do not belong to us; they belong to God. We were not created to be symbols of excess. The base emotion underlying lewdness is usually hurt, with the practitioner seeking attention. The more attention you get, the more you will want. The lack of love and value in peoples' lives drive them to seek attention in destructive ways that distract them from discovering the love of God.

Idolatry is defined as the worship of idols or excessive devotion to, or reverence for, some person or thing. An idol is anything that replaces the one, true God. The most prevalent form of idolatry in Biblical times was the worship of images that were thought to embody the various pagan deities. But in our society, we commit idolatry in other ways when we put people and/or things before God. Some people worship their spouses, their children, their pastors, their jobs, material things, some even their past. God is not second to anyone or anything.

When you take your last breath, you will not be able to take anyone or anything with you. At death, it will be just you and your Creator. We are reminded in Matthew 6:33 to "seek first the kingdom of God and his righteousness, and all these things will be added to you." This verse seems simple enough, but really it is the essence of our existence. We are to put God first and to live life as directed by Him and if we do, He will be faithful and add our desires to our lives. But we can't seek God or His righteousness without first discovering His love for us and the purpose He has for our life.

Sorcery is defined as not only occultism (belief in or study of the action or influence of supernatural or supernormal powers), but also the use of mind-altering drugs (cocaine, heroin, methamphetamine, ecstasy, marijuana, and others; and the abuse of hallucinogenic prescription drugs). Mind-altering drugs are any chemical substance that changes a person's brain function and results in altering their perceptions, mood or consciousness.

Belief in the occult, the use of illegal mind-altering drugs and the abuse of hallucinogenic prescription drugs is the devil's poor substitution for power. When you are involved in the occult or taking mind-altering drugs, your mind and life are not your own. You are only a vessel being used by the devil as a means to an end. However, it is written that the devil will not succeed (Matthew 16:18, Revelation 12:8), so any such activity is a waste of time and money on your part.

Hatred is defined as to dislike intensely or passionately; feel extreme aversion or hostility toward; to detest. I don't know if it is our access to technology and the 24/7 media or what is going on in our world today, but there is a lot of hate in the world. The hate is not out there on its own, it has to be activated by people. People are the catalyst for hate. People hate because they fear unfamiliar people, things and even change.

Hate is such an easy distraction for the devil to use. If he can get you to be afraid, insecure, uncertain, jealous, prideful, ungrateful, and pious, he can easily get you to hate. I can remember hating two or three people; but before I arrived at hating someone, I was first angry with them. If not addressed and healed, anger is a slippery slope to hatred (Ephesians 4:26-7).

As I have mentioned, I spent a good portion of my life being angry. And, from time to time, I still get angry, but it is definitely not like it was before, but it is still anger. When I catch myself being angry, I remind myself that my anger is driven by my expectations that did not occur as I desired. What I need to do is change my expectations and my anger will go away. If I have no anger, I will have no hate.

Each time you find yourself getting angry, I suggest that you try changing your thoughts of what you expected to occur and replacing it with positive thoughts (Philippians 4:8) and your anger will subside. As I said before, people are the catalyst for hate. If we make the effort to change our expectations, we can be successful in subduing anger and hate in our lives and the world we live in.

Contentions are defined as something (such as a belief, opinion, or idea) that is argued or stated; anger and disagreement.

Something I have always tried to avoid are conversations about inane topics that have been discussed a million times, have little value, and seem to be the cause of arguments, disagreement, and hurt. For example: the value of dark-skinned people and light-skinned people, good hair over bad hair, he said she said, who is cheating with whom, and the like.

Instead of inane conversations, we need to increase our knowledge by reading more and participating in social media less, further our education and training, and study the Bible more. Maybe with more knowledge and understanding we can engage in more fruitful conversations that will encourage and lift us up mentally and spiritually.

Jealousies are defined as intolerant of rivalry or unfaithfulness; disposed to suspect rivalry or unfaithfulness; hostile toward a rival or one believed to enjoy an advantage. Jealousy can make you a small person spiritually. A jealous person will continually look on his friend's plate and ask for what they have rather than **FIRST** enjoy what he has on his own plate. A jealous person is so busy looking at another person's attributes and/or accomplishments (appearance, wealth, personality, family situation, and job) that he cannot focus on his own.

Jealous people have not established their identity; they don't know what they were created for, so they long for what someone else has rather than spend their energy cultivating their own value. It is okay to like or appreciate what someone else has; however, we are not to desire what another has to the point where we carry hate in our hearts, mind, or body because we want what they have.

God provides for us all. He gives some people more and He gives some less based on His will. The point is not the quantity or quality of what He gives, but what we do with what He gives us (love, talent, blessings, grace, mercy, favor, and much more).

Remember, God knew exactly what He wanted you to look like, your disposition to be, and your wealth before you were even born. The attributes you have were designed specifically for you, and no one else, to be used to fulfill God's purpose in this life. If you desire more, then ask God for more and have faith that He will give you what you want because you are faithful and He will answer your prayer. But remember, faith without works is dead; that means that you have to work on your situation and God will do the rest.

Outbursts of wrath is when people allow their anger to show itself, explode, and then calm down. After the explosion, they generally feel better. Unfortunately, they usually forget about the people whom they hurt during their outburst.

An obvious example are people who have short tempers and say whatever they want without thinking. This can include parents who, finding themselves ill-equipped, stressed out, or overwhelmed, lash out in words or actions against their children.

I was impatient and had a temper. I would go from zero to sixty in a second if I felt someone had said the wrong thing to me or treated me unfairly. I wasn't raised that way, but because of rejection and living my adult life in fear, it was a way for me to reclaim my value by taking back what I thought someone was trying to take from me. And, I made certain with my words and threats that the guilty person would think twice about trying to hurt me again. All the anger and hurt from my past continually displayed itself in my speech, body language, actions, relationships, how people perceived me and how I perceived myself. With grace and revelation into the root cause of my anger and hurt, God has removed my quick temper. There are still times when I am tempted to respond in anger, but God has restored my heart and I try very hard not to behave as I once did.

Words are powerful. They can lift us up, comfort us, motivate us, direct us, encourage us; they can also beat us down, damage us, and even destroy our spirits. I believe that when babies are born, they are essentially blank pages and that parents and family members are responsible for raising their children to be excellent students, adults, and citizens of their communities. Also, parents are to protect their children from harm and danger, but also guard and protect their spirits. My son Elijah has a beautiful spirit. I remember when Elijah was about nine years old, he told me I yelled at him too much and that I did not listen to what he had to say. I heard him that day, and I realized he was right. My words and anger were affecting our relationship and were becoming an example of how he spoke and responded to other children. I immediately began to change my behavior with my son, and communicated with him in a calm voice and told him what I wanted rather than yell, stressing him out and damaging his spirit.

We all get stressed. We live in a fast-paced world full of obligations and deadlines. Many of us are struggling spiritually, emotionally, physically, mentally, and financially. Then, add the responsibility of raising a child/children, and it can sometimes be overwhelming and stressful. However, we can all do better communicating with others, and especially with our children.

What we say and do has power and we all have to account for the words we choose to use (Ephesians 4:29, Matthew 12:36-37). That power can be negative and it can be powerful. We have all experienced moments as a child and even an adult where our spirits were wounded by what someone said or did to us. We must take every opportunity to be quiet, to correct our destructive behavior, and choose positive words that bring life, lift up, comfort, motivate, direct, and encourage.

Selfish ambitions are defined as having a lifestyle based on "get"—using and disregarding others on a quest to advance self. The devil is the prime example of this attitude. He allowed his pride and violent discontent to alter his mind until he actually believed he should rule in place of God (Isaiah 14:13).

We live in a culture of "it's all about me and what I want."

Old school is out (standards) and the new school is in ("meism"). What most of us considered to be normal is gone; the "new normal" culture shift prevails.

David Brooks explained this best in an article titled "When Culture Shifts," that appeared in *The New York Times* in April 2015: "We now live in a culture of the Big Me, a culture of meritocracy where we promote ourselves and a social media culture where we broadcast highlight reels of our lives. What's lost is the more balanced view, that we are splendidly endowed but also broken. And without that view, the whole logic of character-building falls apart. You build your career by building on your strengths, but you improve your character by trying to address your weaknesses."

Today there is cultural shift to be transparent, to tell all, to show all, to see all, to know all. I sometimes wonder if this momentum is really about people getting what they want without considering the effects of their actions on others. For example, if I see a woman on a regular day just out and about, who is dressed in an overly provocative way or dressed in a way that I can see her breasts spilling out of her blouse, or pants so tight I can see the outline of her personal "jewels," or shorts that cut into her butt, I think she is pushing her own agenda of "look at me, pay attention to me, I have value." In reality, her selfish actions are really saying that she doesn't know her value and she is looking for another person's attention to validate her. Furthermore, her behavior doesn't just impact her. It also influences young girls who see her displaying her body and the attention she gets into thinking that this is a way to validate themselves.

Another example is a single woman who pushes her child's father to participate in the child's life when the father does not want to or have the disposition or skill set to watch or raise a child. The woman drives her selfish agenda of forcing the man to watch the child (because she feels the man owes her or she wants to continue the relationship under the pretense of the child) and in the man's frustration, anger, and fear, he harms, abuses, or kills the child. The woman was not driving her agenda for the benefit of the man or her child, but because of what she wanted. A man who is whole and self-sufficient does not need to be coerced into taking care of his children; he knows and accepts his responsibility and duty as a dad.

My final example is a man who by choice and not circumstances, chooses not to provide for his children. Instead he uses his time, energy, and finances to establish a separate life outside of his children. Or if he is involved in their lives, he chooses not to support his children emotionally and/or financially and may even hurt or kill them.

Too often in our broken culture, men impregnate women but do not consider loving or taking care of the resulting children. Some men are simple-minded and believe that their ability to impregnate a woman is a badge of manhood.

During the past twenty years or so, our society has watered down the importance of God and marketed this new normal of "meism." Some people only see what is in front of them and focus on what they want without fully considering how their actions will affect others.

I believe that self-ambition/selfishness is built on pride and fear. God does not like a prideful heart and He did not create us with the spirit of fear. Fear is a tool of the devil. Self-ambition and selfishness are tools the devil uses to distract us and lead us to sin which puts more distance between us and God.

In each example I gave, selfishness was driven by a person looking for attention and validation, and in their frustration they turned to sin. The solution, of course, is to allow God to love and define your value, rather than conforming to the world.

Dissensions are defined as disagreement in opinion, usually of a violent character, producing warm debates or angry words; contention in words; partisan and contentious divisions; breach of friendship and union; strife; discord; quarrel. When I was an unbeliever, I enjoyed arguing. I did not typically start arguments, but I enjoyed participating in them. I would feel a sense of pride when I won an argument and forced my opinions on others.

After an argument, no one really feels righteous. You can't. When we argue, we tend to say things we should not—things lurking in our hearts that we may not even be aware of. Things we would not say if we were calm and rational.

In anger, I have lost friends. I can honestly say I am glad to have lost some, because in hindsight, we should not have been friends in the first place. But there were two or three friendships I lost in anger that I still think about and regret losing.

Dissensions are platforms of pride, fear, and attention. I realize now that I needed the other person to know I was smarter. And when I retold my victories of winning an argument, I had yet another opportunity of telling someone how smart I was. Being an argumentative person never benefited me—but it did put walls up between me and others. The anger, pride, and selfishness in my behavior distracted me.

Dissensions are not good for our spirits or our bodies. Being an angry, argumentative person causes stress which of course causes damage and sickness to our bodies, such as high blood pressure, heart attacks, stomach ulcers, blotchy skin, and other conditions.

Heresies are defined as dissent or deviation from a dominant theory, opinion, or practice. Believers must be careful. For me, a heresy is a distorted reflection of the truth that is a lie.

The Bible is one of the ways God communicates with us. He tells us what His expectations are and how we are to fulfill them. God's Word is inspired by Him. You cannot add or take anything away from it (Deuteronomy 4:2). His word goes out and it does not return void (empty or powerless) (Isaiah 55:11).

The first and biggest liar is the devil, who is fully versed in the Bible and will present a twisted, distorted perception to God's Word that will lead you astray. The best example is of Adam and Eve in the Garden of Eden. The devil spoke a distorted version of

God's Word to Eve and she believed it and then convinced Adam of the same heresy.

Be careful and selective of the church you choose to worship in. You cannot just *hear* God's Word as told by someone else. You have to *read* the Word for yourself and compare it to what you hear so that you stay aligned to God's Word, not a distorted version presented to you.

According to Gordon-Conwell Theological Seminary, roughly 43,000 Christian denominations worldwide existed in 2012. That is a substantial increase from 500 denominations in the year 1800; and 39,000 in 2008—and this number is expected to grow to 55,000 by 2025.

The largest denominations are Catholic (50 million), Baptist (34 million), Methodist (14 million), Lutheran (10 million), Protestant (5 million), and Pentecostal/Charismatic (4 million). There are theological differences between many of the denominations and, after close examination, some don't appear to be Christ-centered at all.

I can't tell you which denomination is the best or closest to perfection. My advice to you is to read God's Word for yourself and pray for discernment, knowledge, and wisdom as you choose your church home.

Envy is defined as having hatred or ill will; to look suspiciously at, in upon; a feeling of discontent and ill will because of another's advantages, possessions, etc.; resentful dislike of another who has something that one desires; and desire for some advantage, quality, etc. that another has.

I believe the difference between jealousy and envy is hatred. In jealousy, you like and covet; in envy a person has allowed their insecurities to manifest into hate and bitterness. Envy can make you a hateful and unstable person. An envious person is someone that looks at another person's circumstances and wonders how they can get what that person has, how they can step into the person's shoes and take what they have, or how they can be that person in that exact circumstance. An envious person is insecure and does not know his or her own value. They can look at another's plate, but when they look at their own plate, they don't see the value that God has placed in them and their circumstances. They have not taken the time to wonder, ponder, examine, dissect, appreciate, dream, or pray about what is on their own plate. They spend their time looking and desiring what someone else has. It is alright to look at a person that is blessed and want the same things, you just cannot let envy be a factor.

When you are jealous or envious of another person, you have an ungrateful and unfaithful heart. In your heart you are not thankful for your circumstances and you do not believe that God is faithful and He knows what is best for you. If you believe Jesus Christ died and rose again to save you and that he is your Lord and Savior, then you can ask God through Jesus Christ for what you want, as long as it is in God's will and you are faithful (that is, you believe and your actions, emotions, and thoughts all agree) what you asked will come to be.

The problem is not God, but you. You have to ask with authority in the name of Jesus, be faithful, and then wait. If you do what God tells you to do, He will do what He says He will do.

We were not created to walk around and be envious of others. We were made to be a reflection of God's image and to be righteous (in good relationship with God).

Lastly, we never know what another person has gone through to be blessed with their current circumstances. Nor do we know what someone has done to acquire all that they have. God blesses the righteous and the unrighteous. He gives to His creations how He wants, in His own time, and in the amounts He desires. Our blessings and trials are measured solely at God's discretion, not ours.

Stop being envious of others and take a long, hard look at your own circumstances, blessings, and trials and be thankful. Next, pray and ask forgiveness for an ungrateful heart. Then, start to thank God for all He has provided you (e.g., love, life, health, family, finances, etc.), and then ask God for what you want in the name of Jesus Christ Our Savior.

Finally, be still and listen to what God says. Maybe what you want is not in line with His purpose for you. Maybe your request is motivated by an unclean heart. Maybe it is not the right time. Maybe He is keeping you away from something or someone that is harmful to you physically and/or spiritually. Maybe He knows you are not ready to handle what you asked for. It really doesn't matter how you feel about it because your life is not yours, nor is it about you. It is about God.

Murder: The command, do not kill seems easy enough for us to understand. Even so, countless people have murdered someone. In the Bible, in the book of Genesis, it notes Cain as the original murderer when he killed his brother, Abel. In Matthew 5:22, Jesus used three other variations of murder that we engage in without knowing and are progressively worse:

1. Anger and flying into a rage

2. Speaking with a tone and remarks of contempt arising from anger

3. Calling someone a fool ("fool" as used by Christ, meaning morally worthless; a scoundrel; a person who lives an immoral life)

The example of calling someone a fool is equivalent to destroying the person's reputation, character, and name. I want to add another dimension to that, something that is prevalent in our "meism" culture: cursing and calling people derogatory words. I suspect all of us have witnessed someone being cursed out. At the time, we may have thought it was entertaining (e.g., reality shows, neighbors arguing, etc.) or even necessary. In fact, we may have at one time or another been a recipient or even the one demonstrating this behavior.

Before I discovered my value, I was not the type of person who would allow someone to talk over me or curse me out. That was my job. I was typically the one doing the cursing. However, there have been times when I was on the receiving end as well.

Years ago, I dated a man with a broken spirit that was the result of a messed up childhood: abandoned by his father and distant with his mother. This man was intelligent, but lacked self-esteem. Well, as two broken vessels, we had a difficult time communicating with each other like rational adults. Subsequently, there were a lot of hurtful words and cursing between us. We murdered each other with our anger and our words. Even now, when I think about him, there is a hesitancy in my spirit that reminds me of our hurtful experiences.

Not long ago, as I was walking through a parking lot, I heard a young man loudly cursing on his cell phone. As I walked away, each of the curse words he said seemed to float in the air, enter my ears, and poke at my spirit. Words are powerful.

I also want to discuss the use of derogatory words that are common in our society, the N-word, B-word, M-word and others that are casually used to demean people. I am a strong believer that you should not use words in conversation or writing if you don't know what they mean. I challenge you to look up those words in the dictionary and tell me how disgusting they are. People use them to describe each other in anger; casually; and, some say, as an expression of affection, which I never understood.

Take the N-word, for example. It is probably the most offensive word in the English language, yet it is prevalent in our conversation, hip-hop music, movies, TV shows, social media, and in print. The N-word is defined as a contemptuous term used to refer to a black person. These days, blacks, whites, and other nationalities use the N-word to describe themselves and others. When I think of the N-word, I visualize a dead, beaten black man or woman marked with deep scars over their body from being whipped and tortured. Now, why would anyone call their friend, or even worse, a child, a word that is foul, offensive, derogatory, and so hurtful?

The first person I recall ever saying the N-word to me was a three-year-old I was helping to care for years ago. What does a three-year-old know about the N-word? She knows that her mother said it to her and that it was okay to say it to someone else. What does that say about the person who supposedly loved her?

Words come from our hearts to our minds and out of our mouths. Be careful of the words you speak and those you allow spoken in your presence. Words are powerful. Words can set your tone physically, mentally, and spiritually. Negative words make you a prisoner even when there are no walls. Positive words lift you up beyond your circumstances. Spiritual words encourage, heal, and comfort.

Drunkenness is self-explanatory. Its essence is when you are drunk or high, you are not in control of your mind, body, or spirit. When you are not in control, all kinds of bad things can happen. We all see the news where drunk drivers have injured or killed people and in the process have taken people away from their families and friends.

I believe that most people who abuse alcohol and drugs do so to escape from something hurtful that happened in their lives. The alcohol and drugs are a distraction to buffer or numb their feelings from their hurt. Out of fear, they have chosen not to acknowledge and/or confront what that hurtful event has done to them. Instead, they use the alcohol and drugs as a means to forget.

But they can't really forget, because the hurt is embedded in their spirit. The only way they can move forward to renew and reclaim their life is to acknowledge and confront their fear and hurtful past.

The devil uses our weaknesses and speaks to our spirit either directly or through others (spiritual warfare) telling us that we are unlovable, worthless, unfixable, and damaged beyond redemption. These messages are played over and over, eventually distracting us and eventually our emotions are filled with hurt and anger and we seek out substitutes (alcohol, drugs) for God's love.

You must know there is no substitute on this earth or in Heaven for God's love. God's love for His children answers all, restores all, heals all, and covers all (Luke 15:20).

Our lives are temporary, they are but a puff of vapor that appears for a little while then disappears (James 4:13-16). However, in our arrogance, we think we can plan our lives. Not so. God plans our lives and the purpose He created for us to fulfill. Sins are available to distract us and lead us to guilt and condemnation. When we live a life of sin, we are living below God's expectations for us. We are fearfully and wonderfully made by God to do His will (Palm 139:14). This cannot happen when we live a life full of distractions.

Below is a selection of Bible passages for your reading and reflection. I encourage you to read each Scripture noted in this book in a study Bible, so you can gain additional revelation and encouragement.

JAMES 4:17 (ESV)
[17]So whoever knows the right thing to do and fails to do it, for him it is sin.

ROMANS 8:5–8 (ESV)
[5]For those who live according to the flesh set their minds on the things of the flesh, but those who live according to the Spirit set their minds on the things of the Spirit. [6]For to set the mind on the flesh is death, but to set the mind on the Spirit is life and peace. [7]For the mind that is set on the flesh is hostile to God, for it does not submit to God's law; indeed, it cannot. [8]Those who are in the flesh cannot please God.

JAMES 4:13–16 (ESV)

[13]Come now, you who say, "Today or tomorrow we will go into such and such a town and spend a year there and trade and make a profit"— [14]yet you do not know what tomorrow will bring. What is your life? For you are a mist that appears for a little time and then vanishes. [15]Instead you ought to say, "If the Lord wills, we will live and do this or that." [16]As it is, you boast in your arrogance. All such boasting is evil.

MARK 7:21–23 (ESV)

[21]For from within, out of the heart of man, come evil thoughts, sexual immorality, theft, murder, adultery, [22]coveting, wickedness, deceit, sensuality, envy, slander, pride, foolishness. [23]All these evil things come from within, and they defile a person."

GALATIANS 5:19–21 (NKJV)

[19]Now the works of the flesh are evident, which are: adultery, fornication, uncleanness, lewdness, [20]idolatry, sorcery, hatred, contentions, jealousies, outbursts of wrath, selfish ambitions, dissensions, heresies, [21]envy, murders, drunkenness, revelries, and the like; of which I tell *you* beforehand, just as I also told you in time past, that those who practice such things will not inherit the kingdom of God.

PROVERBS 6:16–19 (ESV)

[16]There are six things that the Lord hates, seven that are an abomination to him: [17]haughty eyes, a lying tongue, and hands that shed innocent blood, [18]a heart that devises wicked plans, feet that make haste to run to evil, [19]a false witness who breathes out lies, and one who sows discord among brothers.

1 CORINTHIANS 6:18 (ESV)

[18]Flee from sexual immorality. Every other sin a person commits is outside the body, but the sexually immoral person sins against his own body.

1 CORINTHIANS 6:9–10(ESV)

[9]Or do you not know that the unrighteous will not inherit the kingdom of God? Do not be deceived: neither the sexually immoral, nor idolaters, nor adulterers, nor men who practice homosexuality, [10]nor thieves, nor the greedy, nor drunkards, nor revilers, nor swindlers will inherit the kingdom of God.

1 TIMOTHY 1:9–10 (ESV)

[9]understanding this, that the law is not laid down for the just but for the lawless and disobedient, for the ungodly and sinners, for the unholy and profane, for those who strike their fathers and mothers, for murderers, [10]the sexually immoral, men who practice homosexuality, enslavers, liars, perjurers, and whatever else is contrary to sound doctrine,

1 CORINTHIANS 6:12–19 (ESV)

[12]"All things are lawful for me," but not all things are helpful. "All things are lawful for me," but I will not be dominated by anything. [13]"Food is meant for the stomach and the stomach for food"—and God will destroy both one and the other. The body is not meant for sexual immorality, but for the Lord, and the Lord for the body. [14]And God raised the Lord and will also raise us up by his power. [15]Do you not know that your bodies are members of Christ? Shall I then take the members of Christ and make them members of a prostitute? Never! Or do you not know that he who is joined to a prostitute becomes one body with her? For, as it is written, "The two will become one flesh." [17]But he who is joined to the Lord becomes one spirit with him. [18]Flee from sexual immorality. Every other sin a person commits is outside the body, but the sexually immoral person sins against his own body. [19]Or do you not know that your body is a temple of the Holy Spirit within you, whom you have from God? You are not your own,

JAMES 4:1–10 (ESV)

[1]What causes quarrels and what causes fights among you? Is it not this, that your passions are at war within you? [2]You desire and do not have, so you murder. You covet and cannot obtain, so you fight and quarrel. You do not have, because you do not ask. [3]You ask and do not receive, because you ask wrongly, to spend it on your passions. [4]You adulterous people! Do you not know that friendship with the world is enmity with God? Therefore whoever wishes to be a friend of the world makes himself an enemy of God. [5]Or do you suppose it is to no purpose that the Scripture says, "He yearns jealously over the spirit that he has made to dwell in us"? [6]But he gives more grace. Therefore it says, "God opposes the proud, but gives grace to the humble." [7]Submit yourselves therefore to God. Resist the devil, and he will flee from you. [8]Draw near to God, and he will draw near to you. Cleanse your hands, you sinners, and purify your hearts, you double-minded. [9]Be wretched and mourn and weep. Let your laughter be turned to mourning and your joy to gloom. [10]Humble yourselves before the Lord, and he will exalt you.

REVELATION 21:8 (ESV)

[8]But as for the cowardly, the faithless, the detestable, as for murderers, the sexually immoral, sorcerers, idolaters, and all liars, their portion will be in the lake that burns with fire and sulfur, which is the second death."

JOHN 4:16–18 (ESV)

[16]Jesus said to her, "Go, call your husband, and come here." [17]The woman answered him, "I have no husband." Jesus said to her, "You are right in saying, 'I have no husband'; [18]for you have had five husbands, and the one you now have is not your husband. What you have said is true."

MATTHEW 7:3–5 (ESV)

³Why do you see the speck that is in your brother's eye, but do not notice the log that is in your own eye? ⁴Or how can you say to your brother, 'Let me take the speck out of your eye,' when there is the log in your own eye? ⁵You hypocrite, first take the log out of your own eye, and then you will see clearly to take the speck out of your brother's eye.

ROMANS 8:13 (ESV)

¹³For if you live according to the flesh you will die, but if by the Spirit you put to death the deeds of the body, you will live.

INTERACTIVE APPLICATION

1. Being in denial is a choice. Describe at least one issue in your life that you have chosen to be in denial about.

2. Read Galatians 5:19–20 again. Do you see any of your past and current behaviors described there? If so, please reflect on each works of the flesh that you participated in. What motivated your actions?

3. Do you carry any guilt or condemnation that is keeping you from establishing/re-establishing your relationship with God? If yes, what is it?

4. Can you see a correlation between your hurt and the works of flesh you participated in?

5. Any thoughts you would like to remember later? If so, write them down here.

FOUR

The Devil's Distractions That Prevent You from Seeking Your Purpose

Life is full of worries, riches, and pleasures—bills, sickness, hurt and pain, tragedy, busyness, boredom, family, children, spouses, parents, friends, a new love, job and career, furthering your education, vacations, working out, partying, watching TV, social media, videogames, buying stuff (e.g., clothing, cars, house, electronics, gadgets)—all distractions from the devil that can keep you from realizing your value and God's purpose for you.

We spend a lot of time cultivating and maintaining relationships with things and people; both good and bad. Some of us have so many possessions we spend money to protect them, e.g., by purchasing security alarms and insurance, or building fences.

Most people have a long a to-do list for their lives that leaves little or no time for cultivating their relationship with God. God did not create us to complete our to-do lists, but to complete His. God is not a statue in a church or some figure in a cloud. God is real and He created you so that He could have a relationship with you, not watch you run around establishing relationships with everyone and everything else except Him. God must be the first priority in your life, not an afterthought whenever you need help.

I am good at multi-tasking. I am also creative and analytical, so my brain is always thinking about stuff, such as business ideas, a task or project that I want to do, or some topic I want to read more about. Oftentimes I have to catch myself, because I can get overwhelmed mentally and physically being busy with activities that have nothing to do with my true purpose.

I discovered that my busyness was a distraction that prevented me from what should have been my first priority: cultivating and establishing my relationship with God. I sensed God in my life, but I could not hear him through all of the clamor on my to-do list. I truly love my son, husband, mother, father, family, and friends; and most of the time my job (smile), but I had to get an understanding from God that these are not my first priority.

We all have responsibilities, but they should not be our first priority. God should be our first priority. The Bible says: "Seek ye first the Kingdom of God and His righteousness and all things will be added to it." God directs us to seek His Kingdom (i.e., get to know God and His character, discover our purpose in this life, love and help others, live a life that shares the Gospel and glorifies God) and then, after we have sought God, He will add all things (e.g., love, family, health, career, possessions) to our life. God has already provided us with the formula for a blessed life, we just have to believe, step forward (seek), and walk (action) into it.

I love to listen to and meditate on a song by Earnest Pugh called "Wrapped Up, Tied Up, and Tangled Up." There is a verse in the song that says "He's all I need" and in the background you can hear a woman shout out, "All I need! All I need!" When I hear that testimony through the song, my spirit connects and confirms that yes, He is all I need. He knew me before I was conceived, He was there when I was born, and He will be there when I die; and He is my Creator, the One I must answer to. So, He is truly all I need.

You must step back from your present situation and really look at and discover what people, things, activities, and even emotions are taking up most of your time and distracting you from seeking God's purpose for your life.

Now that I am focused on completing my purpose for God's kingdom, I listen to people much better and I discern aspects of their lives without them telling me. I hear the words they say and don't say. I look at how they carry themselves and dress, and I realize that they, like me, may have never even considered that they were born for a purpose.

The devil uses distractions to deter us from knowing God and getting to know Him better. The devil is the father of lies (John 8:44) and he seeks every opportunity, distraction, and emotion to keep you away from your Father in an effort to destroy you. The thing is that people have a perception that the devil is not real (huge mistake) or they expect to see him walking around wearing a red-velvet suit. The devil is real, he is subtle, and he is patient. He comes at you through people, things, and situations wrapped up to look like what you wanted, or in a manner to soothe an emotional wound—but his goal is always to distract you.

We live in a world that is constantly throwing new gadgets, social issues, problems, and obstacles at us. Most of the time we have so much stuff in front of us, so much on our minds, so many responsibilities and goals, so many things we want to do, so many people pulling at us and taking our energy that we cannot see God through all the clutter we have unwittingly allowed the devil to put in our lives. I realized I could not serve two masters; so, ultimately I had to choose one. I chose God.

When you live a lifestyle that does not acknowledge God or agree with His Word, then you have made the choice that you will serve the devil. You don't have to profess with your mouth that you serve the devil, how you see yourself and treat people says it for you.

Seeking God's kingdom is not a lifestyle where you have one part of your life serving the devil and another part serving God. I am not saying that we are to be perfect or should judge others as they struggle in their relationship with God, rather I am saying that after we confess our love of Jesus Christ as our Lord, we need to act out our faith with works (things and activities we do that represent our belief). Our confession and commitment to our faith should result in a renewal (i.e., reset) and lifelong action and works that serve God's purpose. We are all sinners—even Believers who confess Jesus Christ as their Lord and Savior.

Our faith will always be tested. I have failed countless tests, but I have also conquered a few. I could have conquered more, but I did not spend the time to discern what was really going on. When I was angry, afraid, prideful, selfish, coveted, gossiped, cursed, had sexual relationships, did not tithe, when I wanted to be a leader but not a servant, when I spent too much money, etc., I did not realize there was a spiritual war going on for my soul or that I was being tested to produce a testimony. At those times, I was only concerned with what I could see, hear, and touch; so I failed those tests. It was not until I started my relationship with God and He renewed me that I began to see that my old life-style bore witness that I had been serving the devil as my master, rather than God.

You must decide for yourself who you will serve—God or the devil. You may think, you are young and have a lot of time on your side, but babies and children are dying every day. So, stop! Thoughts like this are the devil talking to you. You may think you are too old, that your time has passed. Stop! That is the devil speaking to you. You may think you have a few things you want to accomplish or settle before you turn your life over to God, but people die every day on the way to their destinations. Stop! That is the devil talking to you.

God is not concerned with your age, position in life, job title, or what you want to accomplish for yourself. He is only concerned about you having a relationship with Him and fulfilling the purpose He made you for. Remember, that even when you don't make a decision, in essence, you have made a decision. Please, do not let your indecisiveness decide for you.

I pray you will make time to think about what I have written and consider how some portion of it may apply to your life. Below are several Bible verses for you to read. Hopefully they will bring you some revelation. In Luke 8:8, it says: "He who has ears to hear, let him hear." I pray that you hear, that the Holy Spirit gives you revelation on God's Word, and that you receive it and apply it to your life.

ROMANS 8:5–8 (ESV)

[5]For those who live according to the flesh set their minds on the things of the flesh, but those who live according to the Spirit set their minds on the things of the Spirit. [6]For to set the mind on the flesh is death, but to set the mind on the Spirit is life and peace. [7]For the mind that is set on the flesh is hostile to God, for it does not submit to God's law; indeed, it cannot. [8]Those who are in the flesh cannot please God.

1 JOHN 2:16 (ESV)

[16]For all that is in the world—the desires of the flesh and the desires of the eyes and pride of life—is not from the Father but is from the world.

MARK 4:18–19 (ESV)

[18]And others are the ones sown among thorns. They are those who hear the word, [19]but the cares of the world and the deceitfulness of riches and the desires for other things enter in and choke the word, and it proves unfruitful.

JOHN 8:47 (NKJV)

[47]He who is of God hears God's words; therefore you do not hear, because you are not of God.

MATTHEW 16:26 (ESV)

[26]For what will it profit a man if he gains the whole world and forfeits his soul? Or what shall a man give in return for his soul?

LUKE 21:34 (ESV)

[34]"But watch yourselves lest your hearts be weighed down with dissipation and drunkenness and cares of this life, and that day come upon you suddenly like a trap.

2 TIMOTHY 2:22–26 (ESV)

[22]So flee youthful passions and pursue righteousness, faith, love, and peace, along with those who call on the Lord from a pure heart. [23]Have nothing to do with foolish, ignorant controversies; you know that they breed quarrels. [24]And the Lord's servant must not be quarrelsome but kind to everyone, able to teach, patiently enduring evil, [25]correcting his opponents with gentleness. God may perhaps grant them repentance leading to a knowledge of the truth, [26]and they may come to their senses and escape from the snare of the devil, after being captured by him to do his will.

1 CORINTHIANS 2:14 (NKJV)

[14]But the natural man does not receive the things of the Spirit of God, for they are foolishness to him; nor can he know them, because they are spiritually discerned.

MATTHEW 6:24 (ESV)

[24]"No one can serve two masters, for either he will hate the one and love the other, or he will be devoted to the one and despise the other. You cannot serve God and money.

PROVERBS 3:7 (NKJV)
[7]Do not be wise in your own eyes; Fear the Lord and depart from evil.

LUKE 10:38–42 (ESV)
[38]Now as they went on their way, Jesus entered a village. And a woman named Martha welcomed him into her house. [39]And she had a sister called Mary, who sat at the Lord's feet and listened to his teaching. [40]But Martha was distracted with much serving. And she went up to him and said, "Lord, do you not care that my sister has left me to serve alone? Tell her then to help me." [41]But the Lord answered her, "Martha, Martha, you are anxious and troubled about many things, [42]but one thing is necessary. Mary has chosen the good portion, which will not be taken away from her."

1 PETER 5:8–9 (ESV)
[8]Be sober-minded; be watchful. Your adversary the devil prowls around like a roaring lion, seeking someone to devour. [9]Resist him, firm in your faith, knowing that the same kinds of suffering are being experienced by your brotherhood throughout the world.

2 CORINTHIANS 4:3–4 (NKJV)
[3]But even if our gospel is veiled, it is veiled to those who are perishing, [4]whose minds the god of this age has blinded, who do not believe, lest the light of the gospel of the glory of Christ, who is the image of God, should shine on them.

2 TIMOTHY 4:2–4 (ESV)
[2]preach the word; be ready in season and out of season; reprove, rebuke, and exhort, with complete patience and teaching. [3]For the time is coming when people will not endure sound teaching, but having itching ears they will accumulate for themselves teachers to suit their own passions, [4]and will turn away from listening to the truth and wander off into myths.

PSALM 1:1 (KJV)

^{1}Blessed is the man that walked not in the counsel of the ungodly, nor standeth in the way of sinners, nor sitteth in the seat of the scornful.

JOHN 8:44 (ESV)

^{44}You are of your father the devil, and your will is to do your father's desires. He was a murderer from the beginning, and does not stand in the truth, because there is no truth in him. When he lies, he speaks out of his own character, for he is a liar and the father of lies.

LUKE 8:4–8 (ESV)

^{4}And when a great crowd was gathering and people from town after town came to him, he said in a parable, ^{5}"A sower went out to sow his seed. And as he sowed, some fell along the path and was trampled underfoot, and the birds of the air devoured it. ^{6}And some fell on the rock, and as it grew up, it withered away, because it had no moisture. ^{7}And some fell among thorns, and the thorns grew up with it and choked it. ^{8}And some fell into good soil and grew and yielded a hundredfold." As he said these things, he called out, "He who has ears to hear, let him hear."

INTERACTIVE APPLICATION

1. When you wake up in the morning, what is the first thing or person you think of?

2. Do you think it is possible for you to talk and pray to God throughout the day? Why or why not?

3. List the top three priorities in your life. Don't write what you think they should be, but what they actually are.

4. Is there a correlation between the amount of time you commit to your relationship with God and the top three priorities you listed above?

5. If I said to you, God should be your number one priority in life, what would your first response or thought be?

6. Any thoughts you would like to remember later? If so, write them down here.

The Holy Trinity Created You to be a Reflection of Them

When we were growing up, my parents made sure my siblings and I knew what behavior was expected from us. We understood how we were to dress; to speak; and to behave at home, school, and with strangers. We knew that our actions were a reflection of them as parents and the values and manners they instilled in us.

The Holy Trinity (God, the Holy Spirit, and Jesus Christ) created us to be reflections of them. Their characteristics are to be reflected in what we do and say so that when we go out into our communities, when we go to our jobs and when we interact with people it is evident what family we belong to: God's.

God has expectations of His children and His many characteristics testify to who he is. Some characteristics of God are:

> **Self-existence:** God has existed eternally and will continue to do so.

Omniscient: God knows everything and His knowledge is complete.

Omnipotent: God is able to bring to pass everything that He chooses. He has no external limitations.

Omnipresent: God is present in all places at all times.

Immutable: God is unchanging.

Sovereign: God rules His creation and He is free to do what He knows is best for us.

Righteousness: God is always right and fair.

Holy: God is pure and separate from the rest of creation. God is morally pure and eternally free; incorruptible.

Love: God is the genesis of love. He is the source and by Him we experience love.

Transcendence: God is unlike any other being in our existence.

Judge: God is the ultimate judge over our lives.

Immanence: God who is at hand, working through the small details of our lives, present and actively participating in His world.

Merciful: God does not give us what we sometimes deserve.

The three characteristics of God that humans can emulate are to be loving, holy, and righteous.

Recently when I was talking with my husband, I began to get angry because I felt he was not taking our discussion seriously. Typically in situations like this, I get a little perturbed, and if I let it fester, it turns to anger. I walked away from our discussion and I could sense that I was about to go down the road of anger;

then I had a revelation about the image of God. My revelation was that God loved me so much, He thought of me and knew me before the world was created and He wants me to be a reflection of Him, always. God originally created me to be holy and righteous. And I knew I could not be a reflection of the Holy Trinity if I was angry.

Now, I am not saying that my conversion happened all at once, because my flesh still wanted to express itself—but I lingered on the revelation the Holy Spirit gave me and I returned to the mindset that I should have. I remembered that my words and actions should reflect my Father. God does not walk around with an attitude. His character is what it has always been, is, and will be. He is consistent in His Word; so as a child of God, I must reflect on my Father and be loving, holy, and righteous.

Below are two Bible verses for you to read that hopefully will bring you the revelation that God has expectations for His children. As we go out into the world, we are to reflect His Glory in our faith, our speech, our thoughts, and in our actions.

GENESIS 1:26 (NKJV)
[26]Then God said, "Let Us make man in our image, according to our likeness; let them have dominion over the fish of the sea, over the birds of the air, and over the cattle, over all the earth and over every creeping thing that creeps on the earth."

2 CORINTHIANS 4:4 (NKJV)
[4]whose minds the god of this age has blinded, who do not believe, lest the light of the gospel of the glory of Christ, who is the image of God, should shine on them.

INTERACTIVE APPLICATION

1. People can ascertain your mood by looking at your face and body language. What impression or message do you typically evoke when you meet someone for the first time?

2. Write down one thing you did or said in the past week that you wish you could do over. Describe how you would re-do the situation.

3. We all change over the course of our lives (physically, emotionally, spiritually) as we mature and grow older. Describe how you feel about yourself right now (physically, emotionally, and spiritually), in this moment.

4. Any thoughts you would like to remember later? If so, write them down here.

SIX

Lord, Renew Me—Make Me Like You

Some of us know we need to change our lives. Some of us know, but don't want to put in the effort. Some of us are afraid to learn more than what we already know. Some of us are in denial. And some of us just refuse to change.

I was afraid and in denial. I always thought I was a good person. But being a good person did not help me establish a relationship with God. I would read self-help books and listen to self-help tapes—and a lot of what I learned made things better—but the words never healed me. I used to ask my mother and friends about things that bothered me—and often their wisdom helped a great deal—but their words could not heal me. I used to encourage myself and pump myself up with false confidence and bravado—and I looked good on the surface—but none of this healed my spirit.

I thought a nice house, car, and other material things would build my status—but they never added any real value to my life.

One Sunday during services, Pastor Larry discussed how some people are mourning and don't even know it. His words, and later the Holy Spirit's revelation, healed me and opened my will and spirit to be renewed. For years, I knew my spirit was broken, but I just would not allow myself to think beyond the hurt.

I am sure there are persons, events, or situations that have broken your spirit and caused distance in your relationship with God. You may be trying to hide your brokenness like I did, but it is there, in your thoughts, words, and how you treat yourself and others. I could provide a list of examples, but ultimately it comes down to you participating and being cognizant of the symptoms of the brokenness in your life and working backward to determine the source of your hurt.

And, therein lies the problem. Most of us do not want to acknowledge that we are broken because we know it will be a painful experience, so we avoid it. Many of us have secrets, hurts, losses, unfulfilled expectations, shame, guilt, and the like that we don't want to relive or have anyone know about. It is easier to focus on other people, our spouse, our children, our jobs, etc., than to address our pain and guilt. We can dialog and produce a list of things wrong with somebody else but we won't put our brokenness and pride aside and attempt to address the issues that lie under our surface that drive us to think and behave the way we do.

When I finally opened my mind and spirit to the fact that I needed healing, I asked the Lord to renew me; which, in essence, meant I wanted to return to my original condition of being holy and righteous (in good standing with God and in a relationship with Him). When I asked God to renew me, I did not think out the process; which, in hindsight, is a good thing. I did know renewal would result in a change of thinking and behavior; I truly did not know what I was praying for.

Renewal is defined as the state of being made new, fresh, or strong again; replacing or repairing something that is worn out, run-down, or broken.

My testimony of renewal may not be like yours. Your journey to God may be different than mine. I cannot say and it doesn't matter; so don't dwell on the similarities or differences. Focus on your path to God; I share mine only as an example.

My revelation came in tears. I am reminded that in John 15:1–2, Jesus says, "I am the true vine, and My Father is the vinedresser. Every branch in me that does not bear fruit he takes away; and every branch that bears fruit he prunes, that it may bear more fruit." I am a branch (Believer) in Jesus and while I am being fruitful (being active and productive as a Believer), Jesus prunes me (cuts off the excess that is not needed) so that I can bear more fruit (be more effective).

I soon discovered that each revelation the Holy Spirit gave me about my brokenness cut into my spirit. I have never been a person who cried a lot, but each cut the Holy Spirit made caused me to cry. Sometimes those tears were from acknowledging the former life I led; some were for chains that are now broken; some were for thankfulness; some were for acknowledgment of grace, mercy and unknown favor; some were for receiving God's love; and some for when I realized the depth of His love for me. One morning, I even woke up crying.

I believe my tears were the result of the Holy Spirit pruning me and freeing me from a bonded life. In John 15:16 (ESV), Jesus states the purpose of our calling: "You did not choose me, but I chose you and appointed you that you should go and bear fruit and that your fruit should abide, so that whatever you ask the Father in my name, he may give it to you."

You must realize that God has plans for you and you must work towards completing them while you are on this earth. In other words, it is not about you; it is about God's purpose for your life that fulfills his will. Period.

Yes, your real purpose may cause you some pain and

discomfort and cause some distance between you and some friends and family, and may have you look at yourself in ways you never even imagined. But there is no way around it. You have to do the work and you have to allow the Holy Spirit to do his.

You can waste more time living in denial and following false doctrines, but God's Word does not change. It will not change. You were made to serve His purpose. If you are not serving His purpose, you are wasting your time and your life.

Our purpose is to complete the task He has designed for each of us and we cannot even start until we have a relationship with God and discover the purpose He wants us to complete. For me, my relationship with God started when I committed to knowing more about Him and asking Him to renew me.

Although my renewal was initiated that Sunday when Pastor Larry spoke revelation into my spirit, my renewal to look and be like Jesus continues and is constantly in motion as I daily submit my mind, emotions, and behavior to Him and His Word, which is true and does not return void.

I had a desire to learn about God but I did not know how to go about it. At other times in my life, I had tried to learn, but there was so much information I did not know what approach to take. Before joining Family Victory Fellowship Church, I was a member at another church for years and had visited other churches, but never received an understanding of God beyond sin, hell, and blessings. Never in any sermon or Bible study session do I recall being ministered to or taught the concept of discovering God's purpose for my life. This concept of discovering my purpose has been a life changer for me.

In 2013, I enrolled in the Ambassador Bible Training School at Family Victory Fellowship Church. I expected I was only going to learn about God. But I learned a great deal from the class. The teachers were absolutely wonderful and the curriculum was designed to make me not only read about God's Word but to also think about God. In the process of learning more about God, I also discovered things about myself. I found I was weak, selfish, prideful, angry, rebellious, ungrateful, impatient, not compassionate, and insecure. Even though I did not sign up to learn about my weaknesses, God's Word is a like a double-edged sword. It cuts both ways: going in and coming out (Hebrews 4:12). God's grace to allow me the breath and opportunity to read his Word was the going in; the revelation of my weaknesses and faults was the coming out. The Holy Spirit was cutting out all of the things that had bound me and was renewing me back to the image of God.

Renewal occurs with submission of our will, our weaknesses, and our faults to God. After years of living in denial, I did not want to see that I was weak. But when I realized how much God loves me, that he gave His only son to die for me, and that he thought of me and planned for me before I was even born I realized I had no power unto myself. I submitted my problems to Him—and then I realized that was not enough. I had to also submit my life to him—and I did.

Submission comes first, then renewal. Renewal is a lifestyle. It is actively seeking the presence of God every day, all day. Renewal is changing the way you think, speak, hear, act, and react.

I have a playlist of songs (see Appendix B) on my cell phone called "Renew and Strengthen Me." My first song in the playlist is "Make Me Over" by the gospel singer Tonex. It is one of my favorite songs because it speaks to my spirit for renewal.

We all struggle with the two people in our bodies, the one that hungers for the Lord and a right relationship and the other that craves the flesh and to do wrong (Romans 3:23). I love "Make Me Over" because the Believer speaks to God, telling Him that he knows his two sides and sometimes the wrong side gets the best of him, but he wants the Lord to make him over so that he can be like Him. I struggle with the old Brinda; and you are going to struggle with the new you. That's okay. That is what is supposed to happen.

The Apostle Paul struggled (Romans 7:14–25), so I know I am no exception. It is the submission of ourselves to God's will that He seeks. Each submission of ourselves is acknowledgment that He is Lord; He is our creator; He is bigger than any problem or circumstance; He is our Healer, our protector, our Father, our Daddy, Our Friend, and our Comforter; the First, the Last, the All and All; he is I Am.

When I truly acknowledge and believe God is all that He says He is, then I won't live a life of anger. I will stop cursing; stealing; lying; being selfish; and starting, instigating, or participating in drama. I am not suggesting that I will never do any of these things again, because I have and I will, but it is not my lifestyle and I am actively seeking God's presence to live the life He created me for.

Also, I want to caution that you must guard what you allow in your presence because it will impact your life and your relationship with God. A renewed person is uncomfortable around ungodly words and behaviors. Be careful of the movies and TV shows you watch, the songs you listen to, and the behavior you allow in your presence. You will sense in your spirit those things that are offensive and hopefully move away from them. You must guard what you allow in your presence.

My renewal came with submission, revelation and tears. I hope the Bible verses that follow move you to a closer relationship with God and, as you discover more about God and about you, that you are led to seek renewal of your life.

Since my renewal, I have found love, peace, and a lightness of life. I have also found my relationship with God and discovered my purpose (not sure if he has more for me to do, but right now I am focusing on this task). I pray that one or all of the verses below lead you to desire God and to renew your life.

2 CORINTHIANS 5:17 (ESV)
[17]Therefore, if anyone is in Christ, he is a new creation. The old has passed away; behold, the new has come.

ROMANS 3:23 (ESV)
[23]for all have sinned and fall short of the glory of God,

1 JOHN 1:9 (NKJV)
[9]If we confess our sins, He is faithful and just to forgive us our sins and to cleanse us from all unrighteousness.

PROVERBS 3:5–6 (NKJV)
[5]Trust in the Lord with all your heart, And lean not on your own understanding; [6]In all your ways acknowledge Him, And He shall direct your paths.

ROMANS 12: 1–2 (NKJV)
[1]I beseech you therefore, brethren, by the mercies of God, that you present your bodies a living sacrifice, holy, acceptable to God, *which* is your reasonable service. [2]And do not be conformed to this world, but be transformed by the renewing of your mind, that you may prove what is that good and acceptable and perfect will of God.

2 CORINTHIANS 3:18 (NKJV)
[18]But we all, with unveiled face, beholding as in a mirror the glory of the Lord, are being transformed into the same image from glory to glory, just as by the Spirit of the Lord.

EPHESIANS 4:22–32 (NKJV)
[22]that you put off, concerning your former conduct, the old man which grows corrupt according to the deceitful lusts, [23]and be renewed in the spirit of your mind, [24]and that you put on the new man which was created according to God, in true righteousness and holiness. [25]Therefore, putting away lying, "*Let* each one *of you* speak truth with his neighbor," for we are members of one another. [26]"In your anger, and do not sin": do not let the sun go down on your wrath, [27]nor give place to the devil. [28]Let him who stole steal no longer, but rather let him labor, working with *his* hands what is good,

that he may have something to give him who has need. ²⁹Let no corrupt word proceed out of your mouth, but what is good for necessary edification, that it may impart grace to the hearers. ³⁰And do not grieve the Holy Spirit of God, by whom you were sealed for the day of redemption. ³¹Let all bitterness, wrath, anger, clamor, and evil speaking be put away from you, with all malice. ³²And be kind to one another, tenderhearted, forgiving one another, even as God in Christ forgave you.

GALATIANS 5:22–26 (NKJV)
²²But the fruit of the Spirit is love, joy, peace, longsuffering, kindness, goodness, faithfulness, ²³gentleness, self-control. Against such there is no law. ²⁴And those *who are* Christ's have crucified the flesh with its passions and desires. ²⁵If we live in the Spirit, let us also walk in the Spirit. ²⁶Let us not become conceited, provoking one another, envying one another.

2 PETER 1:5–11 (NKJV)
⁵But also for this very reason, giving all diligence, add to your faith virtue, to virtue knowledge, ⁶to knowledge self-control, to self-control perseverance, to perseverance godliness, ⁷to godliness brotherly kindness, and to brotherly kindness love. ⁸For if these things are yours and abound, *you* will be neither barren nor unfruitful in the knowledge of our Lord Jesus Christ. ⁹For he who lacks these things is shortsighted, even to blindness, and has forgotten that he was cleansed from his old sins. ¹⁰Therefore, brethren, be even more diligent to make your call and election sure, for if you do these things you will never stumble; 11for so an entrance will be supplied to you abundantly into the everlasting kingdom of our Lord and Savior Jesus Christ.

PHILIPPIANS 2:5–8 (NKJV)
⁵Let this mind be in you which was also in Christ Jesus, ⁶who, being in the form of God, did not consider it robbery to be equal with God, ⁷but made Himself of no reputation, taking

the form of a bondservant, *and* coming in the likeness of men. [8]And being found in appearance as a man, He humbled Himself and became obedient to *the point of* death, even the death of the cross.

ROMANS 12: 9–21 (NKJV)

[9]*Let* love *be* without hypocrisy. Abhor what is evil. Cling to what is good. [10]*Be* kindly affectionate to one another with brotherly love, in honor giving preference to one another; [11]not lagging in diligence, fervent in spirit, serving the Lord; [12]rejoicing in hope, patient in tribulation, continuing steadfastly in prayer; [13]distributing to the needs of the saints, given to hospitality. [14]Bless those who persecute you; bless and do not curse. [15]Rejoice with those who rejoice, and weep with those who weep. [16]Be of the same mind toward one another. Do not set your mind on high things, but associate with the humble. Do not be wise in your own opinion. [17]Repay no one evil for evil. Have regard for good things in the sight of all men. [18]If it is possible, as much as depends on you, live peaceably with all men. [19]Beloved, do not avenge yourselves, but *rather* give place to wrath; for it is written, "Vengeance *is* Mine, I will repay," says the Lord. [20]Therefore "If your enemy is hungry, feed him; If he is thirsty, give him a drink; For in so doing you will heap coals of fire on his head." [21]Do not be overcome by evil, but overcome evil with good.

ISAIAH 26:3 (ESV)

[3]You keep him in perfect peace whose mind is stayed on you, because he trusts in you.

1 PETER 5:6–7 (ESV)

[6]Humble yourselves, therefore, under the mighty hand of God so that at the proper time he may exalt you, [7]casting all your anxieties on him, because he cares for you.

2 TIMOTHY 2:15 (KJV)

[15]Study to shew thyself approved unto God, a workman that needeth not to be ashamed, rightly dividing the word of truth.

2 TIMOTHY 2:19 (ESV)

[19]But God's firm foundation stands, bearing this seal: "The Lord knows those who are his," and, "Let everyone who names the name of the Lord depart from iniquity."

2 TIMOTHY 2:24–26 (ESV)

[24]And he Lord's servant must not be quarrelsome but kind to everyone, able to teach, patiently enduring evil, [25]correcting his opponents with gentleness. God may perhaps grant them repentance leading to a knowledge of the truth, [26]and they may come to their senses and escape from the snare of the devil, after being captured by him to do his will.

1 CORINTHIANS 10:13 (ESV)

[13]No temptation has overtaken you that is not common to man. God is faithful, and he will not let you be tempted beyond your ability, but with the temptation he will also provide the way of escape, that you may be able to endure it.

1 JOHN 3:9 (ESV)

[9]No one born of God makes a practice of sinning, for God's seed abides in him, and he cannot keep on sinning because he has been born of God.

JOHN 15:5 (ESV)

[5]I am the vine; you are the branches. Whoever abides in me and I in him, he it is that bears much fruit, for apart from me you can do nothing.

INTERACTIVE APPLICATION

1. We have two sides (flesh and mind) we struggle with. As the Apostle Paul describes in Romans 7:14–25, one side (our mind) wants to do God's will, the other side (our flesh) desires to sin. Describe your daily struggle between your mind and your flesh.

2. Is the struggle you describe a symptom or a reaction to a past or current hurt?

3. Do you hold a secret, shame, or any guilt that burdens and binds you? If so, speak to God about it.

4. Any thoughts you would like to remember later? If so, write them down here.

SEVEN

God Created You for a Purpose—He is Intentional

For fifty-one years, I walked around broken and never really comprehending the extent of my brokenness. I did not know that God created me in His image to be holy and righteous. I did not know that His love surpasses any love I could ever experience in this life. I did not know that He created me specifically for His purpose to do His will on this earth. And, that ultimately the purpose he has assigned to me to complete before I die is the value my life.

The life I was living was void. It was a waste of time because I did know my value. I did not know what I was supposed to be doing to align myself to God's will.

I've been told that the two most important days in a person's life are when they are born and when they discover their purpose in this life. I agree.

See, I believed in God, and I went to church, and I thought I was saved—BUT I DID NOT KNOW I HAD A PURPOSE.

One Sunday, Pastor Larry began teaching a series on God's purpose for our lives. I struggled with that series. I had no idea what my purpose was. I knew I was good at managing and organizing things and for the past twenty-five years I worked in a field that encouraged those skills, but it was a profession, not a passion. I wanted to use those same skills to be a leader, but God was not telling me that.

I intently listened as Pastor Larry taught the congregation about discovering their purpose, and I prayed and sought revelation for what God wanted me to do. After the series, I still did not know what my purpose was. I prayed and waited for some great sign to come down and tell me what I was supposed to do. One day, I was thinking about my administrative and organizational gifts and I realized that an administrator is really a servant.

Oh, my flesh did not like that at all. My flesh wanted to be a leader. For a week or so, I was a bit mad at God because I did not want to be a servant. I was already spending 90 percent of my day solving problems and I did not want any more of that. But, as you know, God always wins.

My job was to be a servant, to solve problems, to help, and to think of others above myself. This was a tall hurdle to get over for a person like me who was broken and constantly on the defensive to prove herself. But God directs, and he directed me to a book titled *The Practice of the Presence of God*, written in the 1600s by a French monk named Father Lawrence, who wrote of his simple practice of continually (minute by minute) seeking and meditating on God's love and living solely on faith. That book changed my perspective.

The creation is to continually seek the presence of its Creator and do its will. If my mind is continually set on the presence of God, there will be no space for me to seek myself. I am His creation, a servant, continually emptying myself of thoughts, desires, needs, expectations, opinions, and the like to seek out His love and purpose. In return, He pours His fatherly love, holiness, grace, mercy, favor, protection, and friendship into me to do His will.

God seeks us out and tries to get our attention. If we are smart, we will acknowledge Him in our lives and establish a relationship and discover the purpose He has for us. When our lives are filled with God's Spirit and we exhibit love, joy, peace, forbearance, kindness, goodness, faithfulness, gentleness and self-control (Galatians 5:22-23, the Fruit of the Holy Spirit), we have been reprogrammed back to the original condition God prescribed for us before we were even born (righteous and holy), and now we can do His will.

I can go on and on about this and you could pick out the points that you think only apply to you—and I understand because that is what I used to do. But it is not going to work. God does not want 15 percent, 75 percent, or even 99.99 percent. God wants all of you. An easy way to think of this is to look at the nine attributes of a Christian life that should be exhibited in our lives so that others know we are children of God.

Take a real look at your life. Does your life exhibit **love** (not just for your family and friends, but even the people you cannot stand); **joy** (for me joy is a lightness of spirit and happiness); **peace** (for me peace is when I am centered in God's presence); **forbearance** (patient self-control, restraint, and tolerance); **kindness** (the quality of being friendly, generous, and considerate); **goodness** (the deliberate preference of right to wrong, the firm and persistent resistance of all moral evil and the choosing and following of all moral good); **faithfulness** (to be reliable, steadfast, and unwavering); **gentleness** (sensitivity of disposition and kindness of behavior, founded on strength and prompted by love); and **self-control** (physical and emotional self-mastery, particularly in situations of intense provocation or temptation).

So many of us are walking around brokenhearted and distracted with all the things going on in our lives. All of us are equipped with a spiritual gift (some may have more than one) that God purposely gave us. Remember, though, the gift he gives may or may not be what you are naturally good at doing or what you want to do.

I discovered that one of my spiritual gifts is teaching. Out of that, the Holy Spirit revealed to me that I am to be a catalyst to communicate that we need to discover God's purpose for our lives. That revelation led me to write this book and to speak the power of God's Word. I clearly don't know all that God wants me to do, but I have started. He did not make me for the life I had been living, He made me for this purpose: to do His will and be a reflection of His Glory so that others will know Him as well.

No one can tell you what your spiritual gift is; so don't rely on that happening. I had hoped my pastor could help me discover mine, but it didn't happen that way. Only the Holy Spirit can reveal to you what your spiritual gift or gifts are. In order to hear the Holy Spirit you will need to learn to do two things: be still before the Lord and be patient, (Psalms 37:7). The Holy Spirit speaks and directs us all day, but often we are so busy being us, we don't always hear him. So, as you seek your purpose, pray and ask God with an earnest heart to reveal it to you.

And, just so you know, revelations come in all sizes. Don't think that God is going to send a miracle or a bolt of lightning or perform a spectacular light show to reveal your spiritual gift. For a few people, that might occur, but for the rest of us, the revelation is already in us. God put the ingredients in us when he created us. He is not waiting for you to get ready for him to put spiritual gifts in you, he is waiting for you to activate and use the spiritual gift or gifts that he had in mind when he predestined you to be born. So, don't look for something big to happen. Pay attention to your current situation.

For months, I intermittently prayed for God to reveal my purpose—and to be honest, I was a little afraid because I did not know the magnitude of what God would ask me to do. Eventually though, I realized the devil was causing my fear and that I had to do whatever God created me to do.

One Sunday, when I was in the car with my family and we were just about to turn into the church parking lot, the Holy Spirit revealed to me my purpose. There was no loud crack of thunder or bolt of lightning—but I was listening and I heard.

That was it. So please, don't get stuck waiting for a miracle or prophetic word. God has already designed you specifically for His purpose. He has given you the ability to complete the task(s) and He has given you the power and authority, through the power and authority of Jesus Christ, his Son, to complete the task. The only element holding up this process is you.

Imagine how this world would be if we all knew our purpose and we all walked this earth filling those purposes. There would be less crime, hurt, and sickness; and more love, peace, and understanding.

My life changed when I discovered my purpose. My attitude changed, my relationships with people changed, my desires changed, and how I think about myself changed. I definitely am not perfect and I practice submitting my will throughout the day, but I have grown spiritually and the quality of my life is so much better. And, as I walk in my purpose, people I come in contact with get a piece of that love and, hopefully, are impacted in a positive way.

I pray that the Scriptures you are about to read bring revelation into your life and convince your spirit to seek out your purpose. Ask God for discernment, knowledge, and wisdom as you seek your purpose. God wants us to seek him; and in doing so, we will discover His limitless love and His plans for our lives. But first, we must seek, ask, and then listen.

2 TIMOTHY 1:9 (NKJV)
9who has saved us and called us with a holy calling, not according to our works, but according to His own purpose and grace which was given to us in Christ Jesus before time began,

EXODUS 9:16 (ESV)

¹⁶But for this purpose I have raised you up, to show you my power, so that my name may be proclaimed in all the earth.

ROMANS 8:28 (ESV)

²⁸And we know that for those who love God all things work together for good, for those who are called according to his purpose.

EPHESIANS 1:11 (NKJV)

¹¹In Him also we have obtained an inheritance, being predestined according to the purpose of Him who works all things according to the counsel of His will,

ROMANS 12:1 (NKJV)

¹²I beseech you therefore, brethren, by the mercies of God, that you present your bodies a living sacrifice, holy, acceptable to God, *which is* your reasonable service.

MATTHEW 5:13–16 (ESV)

¹³"You are the salt of the earth, but if salt has lost its taste, how shall its saltiness be restored? It is no longer good for anything except to be thrown out and trampled under people's feet. ¹⁴"You are the light of the world. A city set on a hill cannot be hidden. ¹⁵Nor do people light a lamp and put it under a basket, but on a stand, and it gives light to all in the house. ¹⁶In the same way, let your light shine before others, so that they may see your good works and give glory to your Father who is in Heaven.

ACTS 20:24 (NKJV)

²⁴But none of these things move me; nor do I count my life dear to myself, so that I may finish my race with joy, and the ministry which I received from the Lord Jesus, to testify to the gospel of the grace of God.

INTERACTIVE APPLICATION

1. Do you know what your purpose is for this life? If so, please describe it.

2. For those who know their purpose, are you pursuing God's purpose for your life? If so, describe how you are actively fulfilling this purpose. If not, explain why you are not pursuing His purpose for you.

3. Do you tell people about or show them your purpose?

4. For those who are uncertain of their purpose, do you have any clues as to what your purpose may be? Think back on what you liked to do as a child. What did you dream of being or doing when you grew up? Write down your clues.

5. Have any of your childhood dreams (actual or a variation of) been realized?

6. God gives everyone talents. Describe your talents–what you are good at doing, either naturally or by being trained.

7. God gives everyone at least one spiritual gift. Some people receive more than one. A few receive all of them. The spiritual gifts are primarily found in three passages: Romans 12:6–8, 1 Corinthians 12:8–10 and 28–30, and Ephesians 4:11. What are your spiritual gifts?

8. Can you see any overlap between your talents and your spiritual gifts? If so, write them down now, before you forget.

9. Any thoughts you would like to remember later? If so, write them down here.

EIGHT

The Sovereignty of God

The Sovereignty of God is the biblical teaching that all things past, present, and future are under God's rule and control and that nothing happens without His direction or permission. God works all things (you, me, our lives, our happiness, sadness, joy, accomplishments, and tragedies) according to the counsel of His own will (Ephesians 1:11). His purposes are all-inclusive and never thwarted (Isaiah 46:11); He is in control of all.

In Romans 11:36 and Corinthians 8:6, the Bible explains it further that all things are either created, caused, or allowed by God for His own purposes and through His perfect will and timing. The sovereignty of God is not just that He has the power and authority to govern all things, but that He does so in practice as well.

Some people rationalize God out of their lives. If they cannot find a book, person, or class that can answer all of their questions about the existence of God, then they feel justified to assert that there is no God. That is a silly game to play, and ultimately these people will experience their disbelief when they meet their Creator for themselves. God never said He would reveal all of His mysteries to us. Even Jesus Christ, His Son, does not know everything under God's plans. God's plans are revealed under His will and time, not ours.

After a tragedy, people always ask or wonder, why did God allow this to happen? Where is God? Some people grow angry with God and drift away, while others eventually draw closer to God. On the other side of the coin, miracles happen every day: babies are born, people are healed, and millions of people live in peace. The reality is that God is everywhere, all the time. God is with us in tragedy and in peace. He does not show up for the good and then run away for the bad. God is with us always and at all times.

The reality is simply this: God created us and He can do with us whatever He chooses. We can get mad and jump up and down, live in denial and believe He does not exist, choose a false god to believe in that fits our lifestyle and emotions, or believe that God is uncompassionate because He allows evil to exist—but it won't matter. In the end, every knee (that is, everyone ever born) shall bow, and every tongue will confess to God, and each of us will give an account of himself/herself to God (Romans 14:11:12). So, there is nothing to ponder, wait on, deny, or not believe. God is our beginning and He is our end.

In His original plans, God created me for a purpose. He put all the necessary things in me to fulfill His will (holiness) and I was to have a relationship with Him (righteousness). However, that moment of sin thousands of years ago, with the fall of Adam and Eve, changed all of our existences and continues to bind us still. The original sin was the devil, Lucifer attempting to take God's place and be in control, that is be God. That sin occurred again when Adam and Eve disobeyed God's command and desired to be in control, that is be God. And even today, that original sin permeates our flesh as we try to be in control of our lives, that is, to be God.

God created Lucifer for a purpose, Adam and Eve for a purpose, and you and me for a purpose. He created us to do His will and complete His purpose.

We continuously try to be in control of our lives; and to be God. This plan, whether conscious or subconscious, never worked (past), does not work (present), and will not ever work (future). The evidence of our indulgence in the original sin is evidenced in the world we live in and the brokenness of our lives that are on display in our families, the news, social media, movies, TV shows, music and various type of publications.

If we understood that God is sovereign and that He reigns, our lives would be so much better. God looks out for us; He cares for us and He protects us. If we stopped trying to control our circumstances and allowed God in our lives, we could actually have the time to discover our purpose in this life.

I have found that when I step back and acknowledge God as my God, my father, my friend, my provider, my protector, my way maker—I could go on and on with his endless provisions, but when I acknowledge these truths and step out of the way, all things work out the way they were intended to work out and I am free to pursue His purpose. In practical terms, when God is directing my life, I am not living in stress, fear, or strife; and as a result of this freedom, my mind is focused on living a life of love. Subsequently, I am not hollering at my son, I am not mad at my husband for silly stuff, I don't have an attitude when I am at work, I don't mind helping my friend who always seems to call me for help, I don't worry about my mother, or about getting older.

You get the picture. When I truly believe God is sovereign, that He reigns in my life, that I can leave all of my problems and fears with Him and have faith that all things will work together for good because I love Him and I have been called according to His purpose (Romans 8:28).

As I write this, I am certain that as His creation you already know that God is sovereign, that He is King of All and that there can only be one God. My prayer for you (and me) is that every day and every hour we submit ourselves to God, our King, so that we can be free to seek His will for our lives. I hope the following Scriptures are inspiring for you as you ponder God's sovereignty.

ISAIAH 46:9–11 (ESV)
[9]remember the former things of old; for I am God, and there is no other; I am God, and there is none like me, [10]declaring the end from the beginning and from ancient times things not yet done, saying, 'My counsel shall stand, and I will accomplish all my purpose, [11]calling a bird of prey from the east, the man of my counsel from a far country. I have spoken, and I will bring it to pass; I have purposed, and I will do it.

2 TIMOTHY 3:16–17 (ESV)
[16]All Scripture is breathed out by God and profitable for teaching, for reproof, for correction, and for training in righteousness, [17]that the man of God may be complete, equipped for every good work.

2 PETER 1:16–21 (NKJV)
[16]For we did not follow cunningly devised fables when we made known to you the power and coming of our Lord Jesus Christ, but were eyewitnesses of His majesty. [17]For He received from God the Father honor and glory when such a voice came to Him from the Excellent Glory: "This is my beloved Son, in whom I am well pleased." [18]And we heard this voice which came from Heaven when we were with Him on the holy mountain. [19]And so we have the prophetic word confirmed, which you do well to heed as a light that shines in a dark place, until the day dawns and the morning star rises in your hearts; [20]knowing this first, that no prophecy of Scripture is of any private interpretation, [21]for prophecy never came by the will of man, but holy men of God spoke *as they were* moved by the Holy Spirit.

INTERACTIVE APPLICATION

1. Describe the many ways God showed Himself to you today.

2. Do you blame God for something that happened in the past or for your current situation? If so, why do you blame God?

3. If you blame God, why do you feel that you (the creation) have the authority to blame God (the Creator)?

4. Have your feelings caused distance or indifference in your relationship with God?

5. How do your feelings against God manifest in your life (mind, flesh, and spirit)?

6. List the ways God has continued to bless you even though you are angry or indifferent to Him.

7. Make a list of all the things you can thank God for. Then get another piece of paper and write down some more.

8. Any thoughts you would like to remember later? If so, write them down here.

NINE

Continue to Seek and Keep God in Your Life

God never said it would be easy being a Believer; but he did say he would never give us more than we could carry. Every morning when we open our eyes, there are old problems and new problems that await us. There are people we would rather not deal with, jobs we don't always (if ever) enjoy, bills that have to be paid, sickness or injuries that impact us and even our own emotions that we have to deal with. There are a lot of moving parts in our "new normal" society that implies what was previously considered abnormal has now become commonplace. For example, its seems technology changes every six months or so, we have access to news and social media 24/7 everywhere we go, and it seems that opinions on what is and what is not acceptable changes almost daily.

For me, it is a struggle to stay in the presence of God hour to hour when my day is filled with constant movement trying to get everything done that needs to be done including work and looking after my family. When I am in the midst of multiple tasks, I have to stop and remind myself that this is not where I want to be. I want to be in the presence of God.

So, to stay in the presence of God, I have to purposefully meditate on Him and focus on His Word. Sometimes to re-center myself, I meditate on Matthew 6:33, "Seek ye first the Kingdom of God and His righteousness." But oftentimes, I will grab my cell phone and listen to my playlist of gospel songs that speak to my spirit and my journey so far as a Believer.

You cannot make the journey as a Believer by thinking about God only on Sundays for an hour or two, or a generic grace before you eat. There are 168 hours in a week; two hours, or 1.19%, is not enough time to keep you in the presence of God.

I mentioned earlier that I read *The Practice of the Presence of God* by Brother Lawrence. This book has had such profound effect on me. It is a series of letters written by Brother Lawrence on how he practiced being in the presence of God throughout his days. The key word is *practice*. He consciously chose to focus his mind on God's goodness in whatever task he was doing. Whenever he found that he had drifted off, he would remind himself and enter again into the presence of God. Brother Lawrence described such a joy in being in the presence of God, a longing of wanting to continually be with God.

I experienced so much spiritual joy when I read Brother Lawrence's book. It is liberating being in God's presence, wrapped up in His love, talking to Him, and the Holy Spirit entering into the conversations and directing me. The only way I can describe the feeling and texture of my experience is that it is like when I was a child of about six years old and I had a lightness about me—as many young children do.

I love being in the presence of God. I love the sense of being connected to Him and being covered by His love. I love the effect that God's presence has on me; it is as if I am swept away and all the negative cares of this world no longer matter. I am focused on Him and I can sense His presence all around me. I am comforted and I am at peace. When I am with Him, I can see and understand so much better how I can be more like Him. I can do the things He wants me to do—and I want to do them because I love Him. Never in my wildest imaginations did I ever conceive experiencing this type of love.

When you are so in love with God, you want to please Him. He created us to love and praise Him and when the distractions in our lives are eliminated or re-prioritized, we have a clear line of sight to God and His love. I am not going to tell you it is easy to stay focused. No, I struggle every hour of every day. Even if I spent an entire day alone in my house or church, I would still be distracted and lose focus. That is because the flesh still craves fleshly things. Even in God's house, my mind drifts and I have to make a conscious choice to meditate on God rather than on ungodly things.

Take note: We don't have to choose to think on bad or evil things, they just randomly run through our minds. But, we do have to consciously choose to think about good things and to think about Godly things.

To stay focused on God—or as an old gospel song reminds us to keep our minds stayed on Jesus—you must practice. Practice, just like faith is solidified by doing. That means you have to actively practice meditating on God's Word when your flesh tells you to curse somebody out, when your spouse gets on your nerves, when your employer keeps adding new demands on you without more money, when another driver pulls in front of you on the freeway, when you allow negative thoughts of your past to define you, when you start to get older and everything starts to hurt, and when you are sick or injured. You understand what I am trying to say: staying in the presence of God is not a spiritual force that just takes over you. It is a choice you make of where you want your mind to be and how you choose to live.

Again, it is not easy to avoid distractions, but we can do all things through Christ that strengthen us. For me, as I noted earlier, I have a few Biblical Scriptures and a playlist of songs that I use to re-center myself when I feel I am not in the right place.

When I am way off and I feel some bruising in my spirit, I pray and have dialog with the Holy Spirit, because he knows what is wrong with me when I don't want to admit it or am in denial. I acknowledge my sins and ask for forgiveness in the name of Jesus Christ, and the weight I was carrying is immediately lifted and I can enter again into the presence of God.

In your journey as a Believer, you must discover for yourself what triggers you to move away from the presence of God. So, be alert because the devil prowls around like a roaring lion looking for someone to devour (1 Peter 5:8).

Below are a few Biblical Scriptures, I pray and hope will give you revelation. My favorite is Matthew 6:33. I have found that when I make Him my first thought in the morning and through-out the day (seeking Him) that I am focused on doing His will and not my own (His righteousness) and all my wants and needs will be given to me (added unto me).

MATTHEW 6:33 (ESV)
[33]But, seek ye first the kingdom of God and his righteous and all these things shall be added unto you.

LUKE 9:23 (NKJV)
[23]Then He said to *them* all, "If anyone desires to come after Me, let him deny himself, and take up his cross daily, and follow Me.

PSALM 119:15 (ESV)
[15]I will meditate on your precepts and fix my eyes on your ways.

ROMANS 8:15 (ESV)
[15]For you did not receive the spirit of slavery to fall back into fear, but you have received the Spirit of adoption as sons, by whom we cry, "Abba! Father!"

INTERACTIVE APPLICATION

1. Do you ever question whether God hears your prayers?

2. What was the last commitment you made to someone or a project? On average, how much of your time per week did you spend on this commitment?

3. Make a list of your weaknesses. If you can't think of any, ask a parent, spouse, friend, or a close relative for examples.

4. Do you think your weakness are a wall you put up to hide from God or do you think they may possibly be the gateway to receiving and responding to God's love?

5. Any thoughts you would like to remember later? If so, write them down here.

TEN

My Broad Place

Now that you know a portion of the magnitude of God's love for you—that He crafted you specifically for His purpose; that He gave His only Son as a sacrifice for you so you can be reconciled to Him; and that you don't have to live a bonded life, but live a life of liberty, joy, love, purpose, provision, and favor—what are you going to do? Seriously, in this life, there are only two options: you can establish/reestablish your relationship with God or not. And, for the procrastinators, your decision to not make a decision is still, in effect, a decision.

It is not easy to choose God; especially when you think about all the things you believe you will have to give up, maybe even some family and friends you will decide to leave behind.

And, when it gets to tithing, I know you are going to have a difficult time wrapping your mind around giving God ten percent gross (bring the first fruits) of your increase (wages, side hustles, bonuses, lottery winnings, etc.). I know it seems hard, and it is. I mean, really, you have been believing and acting like you are your own god for years. This new concept that you are not god and that you cannot do all things has probably caught you off guard. But you need to get over it and quickly.

All these years, you have been carrying your hurts and pains with you into every relationship. You have told yourself over and over you were not good enough or pretty enough or smart enough; that you are poor and you can't do any better; you are too tall, short, skinny, fat, sickly, or deformed; not educated—and the list goes on.

You have become comfortable with where you are. You can deal with the situation you are in. You don't want to reach for anything because you are afraid that you will fail, be rejected, or others will laugh or talk about you. I get it. You like being in your hole, because you know what to expect in your hole. You have survived in your hole.

But today, right now, is the time to decide if you are going to choose life with God or death that is, to stay in your hole. Over the years you may have thought several times about establishing/re-establishing your relationship with God, but people, things, your schedule, your past, and even you, have gotten in the way of making a decision. So here you are, again at the crossroads of life or death. It is time to discover your purpose.

I sometimes think back on the time I wasted before I discovered my value and my purpose. But then I realize that God was preparing me to convey this message to you: DISCOVER YOUR VALUE, DISCOVER YOUR PURPOSE. I did not know that I had value to God. If I had known, I would not have done all those meaningless and sinful things.

You have value and God has a purpose for you. That is why He keeps calling you and why the devil keeps blocking you with distractions. Yes, God has given you value, but you must first decide what you are going to do.

Palms 18 is a song David composed before he became the second King of Israel, confessing his love to God who rescued David several times from the hands of his enemies, including

King Saul and brought (delivered) David into a broad place that was spacious, comfortable and had no enemies or confinements. God rescued David from his enemies because David was righteous and lived by God's ways. David calls God his rock, fortress, deliverer, refuge, shield, horn of salvation and stronghold from his enemies who forced David to flee for his life into caves and tight confinements surrounded by rocks. But God frees David from his enemies and confinement and places him into broad place where he is free to live without any constraints from his enemies or concerns of injury or death.

In my mind, I see my broad place ahead of me as if I am coming out of a cave. There is nothing there cluttering up the space or holding me back. It is completely open and there is no room for rejection, fear or self-doubt. Within my broad place, I have room to stretch out and clearly see what is ahead, and what is on each side of me. My vision of my broad place has no clutter, no distractions, and is open and allows me to extend my faith. The openness allows me to see possibilities, to imagine things I never would have thought about before, it allows God's presence to easily meet me where I am. Never in my life would I have believed God would deliver me to my own broad place.

Not long ago, I was grocery shopping and ran into a member of my church and her husband. We spoke a bit and she told me that I had a beautiful smile and to never stop smiling. Her words were special to me because my emotions are easily shown on my face. For the majority of my life, I have had people say a variety of things about my disposition, including: "Smile! It's not so bad!" or "What's wrong?" or "You look so mean."

Now, because I am in God's presence and operating out of my broad place, people see a new disposition of peace, patience, love, and understanding. In this wonderful place where God has brought me, I can do what He has purposed me for. I love my enemies. I give more. I am less selfish. I listen more and talk less. I use kind words instead of harsh ones. I have the power to heal and cast out demons. I am not judgmental. I am not afraid to step out of my comfort zone. I welcome opportunities to help and I look for and open doors God has provided.

In 1 Corinthians 2:9–13, it says: "What no eye has seen, nor ear heard, nor the heart of man imagined, what God has prepared for those who love him." I have no idea what God has prepared for me or the full extent of my purpose. But I do know God wants me to convey to others the importance of discovering their value and His purpose for them—and that is what I am doing. There may be other things He wants of me, I don't know. But at this moment, I am doing what He has given me. If and when He reveals more to me then I will, of course, do as He asks.

I know I must take care to maintain what God has given me. I cannot go back to my old habits and fears, nor let distractions or fear keep me from the presence of God. I must constantly be aware of my personal weaknesses and how the devil may again attempt to use those against me.

I have heard that the devil does not mind us knowing God's Word, he just does not want us living out God's Word. Since I have become a Believer, the devil has been about his business trying to trip me up. And he will continue to do so because I am flesh. However, the difference is I know that my enemy walks about looking for opportunities to devour me. The devil uses the same method to tempt and deceive me into thinking that I can control my life (that I am god); so the majority of the time I am aware and I can prepare myself with prayer and meditation to avoid his traps. But in those times when I fail, I refuse to return to my previous bondage, and with a humble heart I ask the Lord to forgive me for my sins and restore me to a right relationship with Him.

So please, do not think you will never fail, because you will. None of us are perfect, only our Lord and Savior Jesus Christ is perfect. Each of my failures is a testimony added to my faith, each is a story to encourage myself and others that struggle with distractions and sin.

I pray that you allow God to save you from your enemies and take you to your own broad place that He designed and prepared just for you.

Below are some Scriptures for you to read. I hope they encourage you as you move from the past into your own broad place with God.

PSALM 18:16–24 (ESV)
[16]He sent from on high, he took me; he drew me out of many waters.
[17]He rescued me from my strong enemy
and from those who hated me,
for they were too mighty for me.
[18]They confronted me in the day of my calamity,
but the Lord was my support.
[19]He brought me out into a broad place; he rescued me,
because he delighted in me.

[20]The Lord dealt with me according to my righteousness;
according to the cleanness of my hands he rewarded me.
[21]For I have kept the ways of the Lord,
and have not wickedly departed from my God.
[22]For all his rules were before me,
and his statutes I did not put away from me.
[23]I was blameless before him,
and I kept myself from my guilt.
[24]So the Lord has rewarded me according to my righteousness,
according to the cleanness of my hands in his sight.

PSALM 18:16–24 (NET BIBLE)
[16]He reached down from above and took hold of me;
he pulled me from the surging water.
[17]He rescued me from my strong enemy,
from those who hate me,
for they were too strong for me.
[18]They confronted me in my day of calamity,
but the Lord helped me.

¹⁹He brought me out into a wide open place;
he delivered me because he was pleased with me.
²⁰The Lord repaid me for my godly deeds;
he rewarded my blameless behavior.
²¹For I have obeyed the Lord's commands;
I have not rebelled against my God.
²²For I am aware of all his regulations,
and I do not reject his rules.
²³I was innocent before him,
and kept myself from sinning.
²⁴The Lord rewarded me for my godly deeds;
he took notice of my blameless behavior.

1 CORINTHIANS 2:9–13 (ESV)
⁹But, as it is written, "What no eye has seen, nor ear heard, nor the heart of man imagined,what God has prepared for those who love him"— ¹⁰these things God has revealed to us through the Spirit. For the Spirit searches everything, even the depths of God. ¹¹For who knows a person's thoughts except the spirit of that person, which is in him? So also no one comprehends the thoughts of God except the Spirit of God. ¹²Now we have received not the spirit of the world, but the Spirit who is from God, that we might understand the things freely given us by God. ¹³And we impart this in words not taught by human wisdom but taught by the Spirit, interpreting spiritual truths to those who are spiritual.

LUKE 10:19 (ESV)
¹⁹Behold, I have given you authority to tread on serpents and scorpions, and over all the power of the enemy, and nothing shall hurt you.

MALACHI 3:10 (ESV)

[10]Bring the full tithe into the storehouse, that there may be food in my house. And thereby put me to the test, says the Lord of hosts, if I will not open the windows of heaven for you and pour down for you a blessing until there is no more need.

MATTHEW 22:36–38 (ESV)

[36]"Teacher, which is the great commandment in the Law?" [37]And he said to him, "You shall love the Lord your God with all your heart and with all your soul and with all your mind. [38]This is the great and first commandment.

GALATIANS 5:22–23 (NKJV)

[22]But the fruit of the Spirit is love, joy, peace, longsuffering, kindness, goodness, faithfulness, [23]gentleness, self-control. Against such there is no law.

2 TIMOTHY 1:7 (NKJV)

[7]For God has not given us a spirit of fear, but of power and of love and of a sound mind.

PHILIPPIANS 4:13 (ESV)

[13]I can do all things through him who strengthens me.

INTERACTIVE APPLICATION

1. What fears continue to hold and bind you?

2. I visualize my broad place as the opening of a cave hidden away in a mountain overlooking blue skies and lush, green grass with pathways that lead to other places just like the image on this book's front cover. Close your eyes and envision your broad place. What does your broad place look like?

3. Any thoughts you would like to remember later? If so, write them down here.

ELEVEN

Discover God's Purpose for Your Life

The second most important day in your life is the day you discover God's purpose for your life. Like most people, there have been days I treasured more than others, like the day my son was born, my wedding day, the day I graduated from college, etc. But none compare to the day the Holy Spirit revealed a portion of my purpose to me. That was the aha moment I had been waiting for all my life. And now that I know my purpose, I don't want to waste any more time doing stuff that has nothing to do with what I understand my purpose to be.

Once you discover your purpose, you have to fulfill it. You may have doubts about how you will do all that God asks you to do, but He will provide you with everything you need—ability, energy, strength, money, opportunity, time, and people—to fulfill His purpose. The only thing you have to do is—have faith and do. God has already handled the rest.

Before we were formed in our mothers' wombs, He gave each of us at least one spiritual gift, some people have more than one.

In Ephesians 4:12–15, we were given these spiritual gifts to pre-pare God's holy people for the work of serving. He gave those gifts to make the body of Christ stronger. This work must con-tinue until we are all joined together in the same faith and in the same knowledge about the Son of God. We must become like a mature person—we must grow until we become like Christ and have all his perfection. Then we will no longer be babies. We will not be tossed about like a ship that the waves carry one way and then another. We will not be influenced by every new teaching we hear from men or women who are trying to fool us. Those kinds of people make plans and try any kind of trick to fool others into following the wrong path. No! We will speak the truth with love. We will grow up in every way to be like Christ, who is the head.

These spiritual gifts were planned for us before we were born, are in every part of our person and have been revealed to us over and over again in our lives. The spiritual gifts God gives and the Holy Spirit reveals are found in Romans 12:6–8; I Corinthians 12:8–10; 28–30 and Ephesians 4:11. They are: Administration, Apostleship, Discerning of Spirits, Evangelism, Exhortation, Faith, Giving, Healing, Helping, Word of Knowl-edge, Leadership, Mercy, Miracles, Pastor/Shepherd, Prophecy, Teaching, Various Kinds of Tongues, Interpretation of Tongues, and Word of Wisdom. I have included a description of each gift in Appendix A. I suggest you read each description and see if your spirit is pulling you to one or more of these gifts.

In my own experience as a renewed Believer, originally I thought my spiritual gift was discernment. After taking the Ambassador Bible Training School class on spiritual gifts, I real-ized that in addition to discernment, my gifts are administration and teaching. So I encourage you to read the descriptions noted in Appendix A and see where the Holy Spirit leads you.

Some advice: don't over-think what God reveals to you. Accept it, receive it, and leave yourself open to meet people you have never met before, to do things you never thought of doing, and thinking in ways you never thought possible. No one can tell you what your purpose is; only God can reveal that to you through the Holy Spirit.

So please, do not ask anyone if they agree with your revealed purpose; including your pastor, spouse, significant other, and best friend. They may be able to give you some insight, but ultimately it is not what they say. It is about what God has revealed to you.

If you are not certain of what you heard or are hardheaded like me, then pray about it and ask the Holy Spirit to bring you revelation. God programmed us for our purpose before we were born, it is already in our DNA, and He has revealed our purpose over and over again in our lives. Some people get it immediately, while others like me live in denial or over-analyze what has been there all along.

Here are some clues I missed:

Clue #1: As a child, whenever my friends and I played school, I always wanted to be the teacher; to organize and run the class (teacher, administration).

Clue #2: People come to me for advice and information (teacher, discernment).

Clue #3: All of my professional jobs have required me to manage multiple projects at one time (administration).

I walked in denial for years as to what my purpose was. I chose not to see, what in hindsight, is now so obvious. My purpose was always there, I was just too caught up in me and my distractions to ever think of using these gifts to fulfill God's purpose for my life.

Think back on your childhood and life. What common thread of gifts and abilities do you recall? What were you really good at that you or someone else convinced you not to pursue?

What are those things that you do so well and that seem effortless for you? If you don't have a clue, then find a quiet place to think about it and pray that God reveal your purpose.

Now this does not mean that you just ask once or twice and wait for an answer. No, you will have to be active in your prayers and meditation. I became frustrated at first, because when I asked God I did not hear anything back. But I was just saying a prayer here and there while waiting for a miracle or some big event to move me.

It does not work like that. God wanted me to come to Him and talk, not just take an idea and run with it. When I came to God over and over in prayer, seeking my purpose, He began to reveal little pieces here and there. And I believe He still has more pieces to reveal to me in my broad place.

So, you have to be an active participant in discovering your purpose. You have to have a sincere desire to know your purpose.

Here are some things you need to do:

+ Pray to God to reveal your purpose.

+ Be receptive and open to the Holy Spirit to reveal your purpose to you (that means, listen and pay attention).

+ Pray some more and listen some more.

+ Be quiet and turn off the noise around you.

+ Be patient.

+ Once you discover your purpose, commit to it with your mouth and heart.

+ Run after your purpose to complete it.

+ Protect your purpose.

+ Be prepared. God may expand your purpose.

Some advice: GET READY!

Now that you seek after or have discovered your purpose, you will find that the devil will take more interest in you. When I was a "good" person, life was just rolling along. Now that I am a Believer and walk in God's purpose, I can see that more drama attempts to unfold in my life. But I realize that there is a spiritual war going on that I cannot see with my eyes.

When you are seeking or have found your purpose this is when the devil will spend more time with you and tell you all the ways you can't do what God told you to do. He will tell you things like: you are too busy, you are too young, you are too old, you don't have the right skills or education ... blah, blah, blah. Stop welcoming the devil's conversation and listen to God's voice that has been calling you all your life. God gave you power and authority, so use it. Tell the devil to get behind you in the name, power and authority of Jesus Christ and keep moving forward.

God planned this moment with you before the world was ever made. He knew you, He designed you exactly the way He wanted, He put into you the specific purpose He wanted you to complete, and He orchestrated people and obstacles in your life for this specific time.

There is no certain way to look, there is no specific educational requirement, there is no particular social status to do God's will. God uses the people He has chosen to do His will. The Bible is full of ordinary people God chose to do His will, like Noah, Moses, Jonah, Ruth, the prophets, the disciples, and so many others. I am certain that many, if not all, had reservations, were afraid, were insecure, thought they were too young or too old, or would not be accepted and the like—but they still completed the tasks they were given and, in the process, helped others move closer to God.

As you start to understand what you should be doing to serve God, I suggest that you RUN toward your purpose. I say run because if you stand still, your flesh will begin to confess to you its limitations and the devil will have time to distract you and make you believe your purpose is something for you to complete later or not at all.

I am running toward what God has for me—I have to. I don't want to waste any more time and I know at the end of my life I will have to answer for many things. When I meet Jesus, I want to hear Him say, "Well done, good and faithful servant. You have been faithful over a little; I will set you over much. Enter into the joy of your master." So, I don't have any more time to waste. Some goals, desires, and aspirations that once vexed me, no longer appeal to my spirit. I have a mission and I am set on completing it.

I pray that something in this book inspires you to begin your journey to reestablish or reassess your relationship with God and in that process you discover your value and purpose. I also, pray that this inspiration will cause you to run toward your purpose. Proverbs 19:21 says, "Many are the plans in a person's heart, but it is the Lord's purpose that prevails."

My purpose is to proclaim that all humans—men, women, and children of all races and status—should discover their purpose in this life and complete it before they die. I am not a Bible scholar and I am not a counselor—but I am a Believer fulfilling what God revealed to me to do. And that is to tell people they have value and that God has a purpose for their lives.

That is why I wrote this book. Hopefully my testimony as I have shared with you in this book will prompt you to answer God's call for your life.

Now RUN! Don't ask questions, don't look back and don't wait on anybody. Pray and run toward the purpose God has for your life.

INTERACTIVE APPLICATION

1. If you have not yet discovered your purpose, do not think God has overlooked you or that you are unworthy. The moment that you are to walk into and receive your revelation—your own aha moment—is just before you. In the meantime, what can you do to prepare yourself to discover your value and purpose?

2. If you know your purpose, are you ready to walk in your purpose every day? How do you know that you are prepared?

3. The devil knows that you are valuable in God's Kingdom. As you operate in your purpose, the devil's handiwork will occur more often and become more apparent to you. Do you sense a more intense struggle in your spirit?

4. Are you content with the purpose God has given you or do you struggle with how the purpose will manifest in your life?

5. Once you accept and commit to your purpose, your flesh will come up with dozens of reasons why you cannot do what God told you to do. What limitations is your flesh confessing to you?

6. Describe your purpose again and explain why it is important for you to complete this purpose before you die.

7. What or who will you allow to distract and stop you from your purpose?

8. Any thoughts you would like to remember later? If so, write them down here.

APPENDIX A

Spiritual Gifts

SPIRITUAL GIFTS HAVE THREE PURPOSES:

+ to equip the body of Christ (that is, the collective body of Believers, Saints) for the work of ministry (discovery and activation of their spiritual gifts);

+ for building up (edifying and maturing) the body of Christ; and

+ to glorify God.

Spiritual gifts are given by God to every human and are controlled by the Holy Spirit. Spiritual gifts are not human talents and abilities. Some Believers operate in their spiritual gifts daily, some periodically, and others only for an appointed time. Some people are called by God to minister and hold office (work part and full time) in their spiritual gifts.

As a Believer you are to:

+ Desire your spiritual gifts.

+ Develop and use your spiritual gifts to equip the body of Christ, build up the body of Christ, and glorify God.

For more understanding of spiritual gifts, please first read a study Bible. Then, to support your learning, read books and articles on the topic of spiritual gifts. There are many study Bibles to choose from. My personal Bible is *The King James Study Bible* by Thomas Nelson Publishers. A book I found helpful in my studies was *The Ministry Gifts* by Kenneth E. Hagin.

For the most part, spiritual gifts are discussed in these Bible Scriptures:

ROMANS 12:4–8 (ESV)
[4]For as in one body we have many members, and the members do not all have the same function, [5]so we, though many, are one body in Christ, and individually members one of another. [6]Having gifts that differ according to the grace given to us, let us use them: if **prophecy**, in proportion to our faith; [7]if service, in our **serving**; the one who teaches, in his **teaching**; [8]the one who **exhorts**, in his exhortation; the one who **contributes**, in generosity; the one who **leads**, with zeal; the one who does **acts of mercy**, with cheerfulness.

1 CORINTHIANS 12:8–10 (ESV)
[8]For to one is given through the Spirit the utterance of **wisdom**, and to another the utterance of **knowledge** according to the same Spirit, [9]to another **faith** by the same Spirit, to another gifts of **healing** by the one Spirit, [10]to another the **working of miracles**, to another **prophecy**, to another the ability **to distinguish between spirits**, to another **various kinds of tongues**, to another **the interpretation of tongues**.

1 CORINTHIANS 12:27–28 (ESV)
[27]Now you are the body of Christ and individually members of it. [28]And God has appointed in the church first **apostles**,

second **prophets**, third **teachers**, then **miracles**, then gifts of **healing, helping, administrating**, and **various kinds of tongues**.

EPHESIANS 4:11–12 (ESV)
[11]And he gave **the apostles, the prophets, the evangelists, the shepherds and teachers**, [12]to equip the saints for the work of ministry, for building up the body of Christ, one **who exhorts**, in his exhortation; the one **who contributes**, in generosity; the one **who leads**, with zeal; the one **who does acts of mercy**, with cheerfulness.

Spiritual Gifts in Scripture			
Romans 12–48	1 Corinthians 12:8–10	1 Corinthians 12:27–28	Ephesians 4:11–12
Prophecy	Word of Wisdom	Apostles	Apostles
Serving	Word of Knowledge	Prophets	Prophets
Teaching	Faith	Teachers	Evangelists
Exhortation	Healing	Miracles	Shepherds
Contributor (Giver)	Working of Miracles	Healing	Teachers
Leader	Prophecy	Helping	Exhorter
Mercy (Kindness)	Distinguish between spirits (Discerning of Spirits)	Administration (Guiding)	Contributor (Giver)
	Various Kinds of Tongues	Various Kinds of Tongues	Leader
	Interpretation of Tongues		Mercy (Kindness)

Categories of Spiritual Gifts		
Gifts of Revelation	Gifts of Demonstration	Gifts of Inspiration
Word of Knowledge	Gift of Faith	Gift of Prophecy
Word of Wisdom	Working of Miracles	Gift of Tongues
Discerning of spirits	Gifts of Healing	Interpretation of Tongues

DEFINITIONS OF SPIRITUAL GIFTS

Below are the definitions of spiritual gifts I have surmised from a variety of sources. For your own understanding of each spiritual gift, I suggest you read and study the Bible, confirm what you already know about yourself, and open your heart and spirit to a new revelation of God's plans for you.

Administration: Those with this spiritual gift guide the body of Christ toward accomplishing God's goals and directives. The Holy Spirit enables some Christians with the Gift of Administration to organize, direct, and implement plans to lead others in the different ministries of the Church. This gift is more directed toward goals, tasks, details, and organization.

Apostles: Taken from the Greek word *aposotolos*, it means "one sent forth," "a sent one." Such individuals are sent by God (commissioned) to be messengers/ambassadors of Jesus Christ. An apostle is also a preacher or a teacher or a preacher and a teacher of God's Word (Timothy 2:7, 2 Timothy 1:11). An apostle's ministry seems to embrace all of the other spiritual gifts, the most distinct is to establish new ministries and churches. Apostles are leaders of leaders and ministers of ministers. Such gifts can be found in church planters, some Christian scholars, and Christian institutional leaders and people with multiple ministries or churches.

Discerning of Spirits: The supernatural revelation from the Holy Spirit with the ability to distinguish between truth and error, to distinguish the influence of God and the devil in a person, statement, situation, or environment. The Greek word for the gift of discernment is *Diakrisis*.

Evangelists: One who brings the Good News; a messenger of good tidings. Their calling and message is preaching salvation through Jesus Christ to unbelievers so they respond in faith and move toward discipleship. The Bible gives wonderful examples of evangelism on an individual level (Acts 8:26-40) and in larger groups (Acts 2:14-42). All Christians are responsible to spread the Gospel. But those who have the spiritual gift of evangelism have an even greater level of responsibility because of the task God has especially equipped them to do.

Exhorter: The gift of exhortation is often called the "gift of encouragement." The Greek word for this gift is *Paraka-leo*. It means to beseech, exhort, call upon, to encourage and to strengthen. The exhorter reminds the hearer of the powerful and amazing work of God in Christ our Lord and Savior. In the Church this gift is used to strengthen and encourage those wavering in their faith, to uplift, motivate, challenge, rebuke, and to foster spiritual growth and action.

Faith: The supernatural ability, given by the Holy Spirit, to believe God's promises, power, and presence without a doubt. The person with this gift can discern the will and power of what God wants to happen and be confident and unwavering in their belief in God's ability to fulfill His purposes, even when there is no concrete evidence.

Giver/Contributor: The Holy Spirit imparts this gift to some in the Body of Christ to meet the needs of the Church and its ministries, missionaries, or of people who do not have the means to provide fully for themselves. Givers encourage, provide, and give all the credit to God's love and provision. The spiritual gift of giving includes monetary help, but also includes a person giving their abilities, resources, and/or time.

Healing: The supernatural ability God gives to some to serve as human instruments through whom it pleases Him to cure illnesses, restore health, and destroy the works of the devil in the human body apart from the use of natural means. Some also think of the gift of healing to be applicable to not just the physical body but also to emotional, mental, and spiritual well-being.

Helping: A person gifted in assisting others with needs.

Word of Knowledge: The supernatural revelation by the Holy Spirit of certain facts in the mind of God. The special ability that God gives to certain Christians to discover, accumulate, analyze, and clarify information and ideas that are pertinent to the growth and well-being of the body of Believers.

Leader: Someone who is gifted in leadership is to use his or her gift with a passion to help people grow in the Lord.

Mercy/Kindness: Those with the spiritual gift of mercy/kindness have great empathy for people in their trials and sufferings and can quickly discern when someone is not doing well. The Holy Spirit gives this spiritual gift to some in the Body of Christ to love and assist those who are suffering.

Miracles/Working of Miracles: The supernatural intervention in the ordinary course of nature; works closely with the gifts of faith and healing. The spiritual gift of miracles reveals God's power through individuals.

Pastors/Shepherds: A minister of the gospel who has the responsibility of a church and congregation, whose duty is to watch over the people of his charge, and instruct them in the sacred doctrines of Christian religion. Pastors are necessary for the maturing and equipping of the local body of saints. The greatest example of a shepherd is our Lord Jesus Christ.

Prophecy/Prophets: Direct utterance of things to people that are not premeditated and not of human intellect but from God. Prophecy should bring forth edification (instruction, improvement), exhortation (urgent communication), or comfort (1 Corinthians 14: 3).

Teaching/Teachers: God gives this special ability to certain members of the Body of Christ to communicate a personal understanding of the Bible and faith to instruct, guide, edify, and nurture Christians in the Word of God in way that it can be applied to life and the building up of the Church.

Various Kinds of Tongues: The supernatural ability to speak in a tongue to God and not to people (I Corinthians 14:2). They utter mysteries by the Spirit which edify the speaker but not the Church. Requires another person gifted in interpreting what is said so that it can edify the Church.

Interpretation of Tongues: The supernatural power to reveal the meaning of tongues. This gift is used in conjunction with that of the gift of Various Kinds of Tongues. This gift is a special ability for certain Christians to communicate a message from God through the Holy Spirit in a language they never learned (1 Corinthians 14:27).

The Word of Wisdom: The supernatural revelation by the Spirit of God concerning purpose in the mind and will of God. This gift involves having a sense of divine direction, being led by the Holy Spirit to act appropriately in a given set of circumstances and rightly applying knowledge. The gift of wisdom is the wisdom of God. The gift of the word of wisdom is not natural and it cannot be gained through study or experience.

APPENDIX B

Playlist

Below are some of the songs I like to listen to when I need to renew my spirit. Have fun putting your playlist together!

"Make Me Over," Tonex and the Peculiar People
"Rain On Us," Earnest Pugh
"Holy One," Anaysha
"Yes" (album version), Shekinah Glory
"Break Every Chain" (live), Tasha Cobb
"Let Go," Dewayne Woods
"I Believe," John P. Kee & New Life Community Choir
"Wrapped Up, Tied Up, Tangled Up," Earnest Pugh
"I Give Myself Away," William McDowell
"I Surrender All," William McDowell
"I Belong to You," William McDowell
"I Need Your Glory," Earnest Pugh
"Perfect Peace," Earnest Pugh

"God Is," James Cleveland

"It Ain't Over," Maurette Brown Clark

"Fighting For Me," Anthony Evans

"Greater Is Coming," Jekalyn Carr

"Imagine Me," Kirk Franklin

"Reveal," Chris Graham

"This Place," Tamela Mann

"For Every Mountain," Kurt Carr and The Kurt Carr Ministry

"Keep Yo Mind," Deitrick Haddon

"My Testimony" (intro version), Marvin Sapp

"Have Your Way," Deitrick Haddon

"Worshiper In Me," Marvin Sapp

"Thirsty" (reprise), Marvin Sapp

"Jesus" (live, extended), Le'Andria Johnson

"It's Working," William Murphy

"I Won't Complain," Rev. Paul Jones

"I Choose To Worship," Wess Morgan

"New Life," John P. Lee and the New Life Community Choir

"For Your Glory" (live), Tasha Cobb

"Lovin' Me," Jonathan McReynolds

"The Best In Me" (album version), Marvin Sapp

"Why," Jonathan McReynolds

"Never Would Have Made It," Marvin Sapp

About the Author

Brinda Devine resides in Oak Park, Michigan, with her husband, Eddie, and their son, Elijah. Discover Your Value, Discover Your Purpose is Brinda's first book and writing experience.

Brinda has worked in the commercial real estate industry for over twenty-five years and holds a Bachelor of Science in Business Administration from Wayne State University, is working toward completing her M.B.A and is a licensed State of Michigan Real Estate Broker.

Brinda and her family are actives member of Family Victory Fellowship Church, located in Southfield, Michigan.